California Coastal Passages

California Coastal Passages

SAN FRANCISCO TO ENSENADA, MEXICO

Brian M. Fagan

Published by
CAPRA PRESS and CHARTGUIDE, LTD.
1981

To Judy,
with much love,
and thanks for sharing so many hours at sea;
and to Lindsay Michelle,
who arrived in the middle.

Cover photograph by Toni Abbott.
Cover design, layout and typography by Terri Wright.
Illustrations by Alyson Nethery.

Library of Congress Cataloging in Publications Data

Fagan, Brian M.
   California Coastal Passages.

   Includes bibliographical references and index.
   1. Boats and boating—California—Guide-books.
2. Boats and boating—Mexico—Baja California (State)—
Guide-books. 3. California—Description and travel—
1951-   —Guide-books. 4. Baja California (State)—
Description and travel—Guide-books. I. Title.
GV776.C22C423   917.94,   80-25968
Capra Press ISBN 0-88496-161-3
ChartGuide ISBN 0-938206-03-6

Co-Published by

CAPRA PRESS	CHARTGUIDE, LTD.
P.O. Box 2068	300 N. Wilshire, #5
Santa Barbara, CA 93120	Anaheim, CA 92801

CONTENTS

PREFACE

California Coastal Passages began as a series of ideas about passage-making in California formulated during fifteen years of sailing off the West Coast. These ideas lurked in the back of my mind for years, helped me plan cruises as far afield as Finland and Greece, and to survive the shallow waters of the Bahamas. Then a couple of cruising seminars came along in Los Angeles and I found myself answering more questions about longer passages in California than about island hopping. What had been pleasurable, and perhaps personal, knowledge now became an idea for a book. The final catalyst was Noel Young of Capra Press, who was his usual persuasive self, full of ideas for an attractive and usable volume. So fifteen years of cruising came between two covers.

In 1979, Graham Pomeroy and I published a *Cruising Guide to the Channel Islands* (Capra Press and Western Marine, 1979), in which we described the mainland coast between Point Conception and Point Mugu, the Santa Barbara Channel, and the offshore islands of Southern California. This is a highly detailed cruising guide, designed for local cruising rather than the passage-maker. *California Coastal Passages* uses many of the techniques employed in the earlier cruising guide, but is designed for a different purpose: for planning and executing longer voyages and extended cruises the length of Central and Southern California.

This book is strong on strategy and general description and light on minute detail, which is available in many other yachting publications. This is a book of qualitative impressions, of ideas and strategies that have enabled me to make successful passages along the coast in a wide variety of weather conditions. I stress the word impressionistic, for good seamanship is based on impressionistic judgments about local conditions and ever changing circumstances of wind and weather. You may end up disagreeing with my judgments, but then conditions may be different when you are in the same place.

California Coastal Passages will be of most use if combined with NOS charts or more detailed publications. I try to give you the general outline and major landmarks, as well as ideas about favored courses, currents, and so on. Charts and guide books give you vital information to find your way around major harbors and small craft facilities.

One school of thought among California sailors believes that you can find your way around very nicely by leaving the Golden Gate and literally "turning left at the lights." Well, you can, but you may have many frustrating moments and sleepless nights. This passage-making guide is designed for people like me who worry about longer passages, and want to know what they are likely to face beyond the traffic lights. To judge from cruising seminars, there are far more of us than perhaps would admit it.

California Coastal Passages is based not only on my cumulative knowledge obtained aboard various sailing vessels, but on a mass of published data and informal knowledge compiled from dozens of knowledgeable people. If there is a model for this volume, it was written in 1858 by the eminent geographer and surveyor George Davidson. He spent years exploring every corner of the California coast in small boats in all types of weather. His *Directory for the Pacific Coast of the United States* became the *US Coast Pilot* we are familiar with today. The *Directory* is an impressionistic sketch based on thousands of miles of "moving continually along the seaboard in every manner of conveyance." This passage guide is an attempt to write a similar sketch a century and a quarter later.

The first three chapters of this guide are general essays on California passage-making, covering such topics as choice of vessel, equipment, and weather conditions. The remaining sections are detailed sailing directions, starting with the Golden Gate and ending in Ensenada, Mexico. These sailing directions are compiled from the perspective of a sailing vessel, since I do most of my cruising under sail. I have, however, made several coastal passages in power boats, which have given me experience from a powerboating perspective. Another assumption I made was that the average small yacht is not equipped with radar, Loran, Omni, satellite navigators, and other elaborate electronic aids. For this reason, I have omitted mention of good radar targets, Loran stations, etc., in the belief that a mass of such information could confuse the typical small boat owner. Both the *US Coast Pilot* and the *Pacific Boating Almanac* provide such data on an annually revised basis. I assume you have a radio direction finder on hand, a compass, a pair of dividers, parallel rulers, and charts. These, and some form of log, are all you need to maintain the dead reckoning (DR) plots vital to basic coastal navigation. Yes, dear reader, I am biassed: electronic gadgets always laugh at me and promptly go wrong. I have assumed that yours do too...

The perceptive reader will notice that I have another bias: a belief that cruising under sail in California is best enjoyed with the aid of a diesel auxiliary engine. I am not prejudiced against purists who say one should do everything by sail. Quite the contrary, I think the skills of sailing in close quarters are grossly neglected. Everyone who ventures offshore should be able to sail their boat to their destination and to their berth under sail if the engine packs in. This ability is a basic safety precaution. Yachts under 22 feet and ultra light displacement vessels that can glide along and maneuver in the slightest air can still go anywhere under sail in safety. But let's be realistic. We Californians sail in congested waters, where the risk of collision in marina and narrow channel is high. Many occasions arise when it is downright dangerous to insist on your rights under sail, however expert a skipper you are. Anyone who has entered Marina del Rey or Newport Beach late on a summer Sunday afternoon will understand. Secondly, we share California waters with commercial and military vessels going about their lawful missions. The Coast Guard and other government agencies have taken extraordinary precautions to prevent collisions, instituting traffic separation schemes, and other controls in the cause of safe navigation by everyone. The International Rules for the Prevention of Collision at Sea are highly specific about the responsibilities of small craft operating in restricted waters. It is our duty to keep clear and to give way to commercial ships wherever they have limited room to maneuver. Thus, to sail up a narrow large ship channel, or to lie becalmed in a traffic lane is not only potentially suicidal, but downright idiotic. Sometimes prudent seamanship in the good old- fashioned sense dictates using your engine, simply to keep out of the way or to maintain steerage way to avoid endangering others. In this day and age your collision rights do not include the blanket "Steam gives way to sail" provision so beloved of bar admirals. So, ship offshore with an engine and use it when needed, even if you are an expert.

It is a fact of life that coastal passages in California almost invariably mean some lengthy trips to windward, to reach a cruising ground, or to return to home base after a leisurely vacation cruise. A few fortunate people have open schedules. But most of us have limited time off, and timetables to meet. Your options are simple: motor to windward and sail when you want to enjoy a change, spending more time downwind, or sail the whole distance upwind and spend your vacation that way. Most of us dislike long beats to windward. I certainly do: I go to sea for pleasure. I suspect our nineteenth-century predecessors would have adored the diesel engine. George Davidson records that a sailing ship used to "be three days working from San Buenaventura to Santa Barbara" in the 1850s. You can tack the same distance in half a day today, but the passage can still be tiresome. If you have any doubts about the advantages of being able to use your engine to go to windward, read Richard Henry Dana's *Two Years Before the Mast.* Unless you are prepared to tack many hundreds of miles offshore, you can count on much of motoring to get to windward. *California Passage* assumes you are prepared to use your engine. Indeed, I recommend many instances when you are best off to do so.

This book expresses numerous opinions about courses to lay, anchorages and harbors to use, and about cruising conditions generally. If anything, these comments are on the conservative side. Please recognize these as my personal opinions. Your judgment as to whether to use an anchorage, make a passage, or shape a particular course must be based on conditions perceived at the time you are there. *In the final analysis, safe passage-making comes down to sound judgments on the spot — and I cannot make these for you.*

California Coastal Passages is as accurate as we can make it at the time of publication. Conditions are changing all the time, and despite every care, some errors or inaccuracies may have crept into the book. Many of the strategies recommended in these pages have never appeared in print before. Interested readers are encouraged, even urged, to bring changes, errors, or different strategies to the attention of the author, c/o Department of Anthropology, University of California, Santa Barbara, California 93106.

—*BRIAN M. FAGAN*

Conventions

Certain arbitrary choices had to be made while writing this book. You should be aware of them as you use this guide:

Compass points are not always written out in full, and appear as N,S,NE,NW, etc.

Bearings and Courses are given in degrees magnetic (1980). Although normal convention is to give true bearings, we felt that a magnetic bearing would be less trouble for small craft fitted with magnetic compasses. Check the variation for the year you use this book, and remember to convert your courses taken from publications that use true bearings.

Distances are given in nautical miles (2000 yards) throughout, even land distances.

Depths are recorded in fathoms (6-foot units) and feet. We tend to give a range, ie. 15-25 feet rather than a spot reading. All soundings are to mean lower, low water. In other words, calculate your tidal depths from our base line soundings.

Lights and radiobeacons. Although every effort has been made to make this book relatively timeless, we have given light and radiobeacon characteristics as they were on October 1, 1980. *Check latest chart editions and Local Notices to Mariners for corrections.*

Light characteristics are given as follows:
Gp.Fl. W.R. 5 sec. 10 miles
(Group flashing white and red every 5 seconds, visible (theoretically)

for ten miles). Light heights are omitted except where significant, but can be found in *ChartGuide*, on most charts, or in the *Light List*.

We normally give the morse and letter characteristics and frequency of radiobeacons. The range is given of the more powerful beacons commonly used in passage-making. Most harbor radiobeacons are limited to about a ten mile range, and, in any case, are of limited use at greater distances. All marine and aero radiobeacons and Omni, principal VHF station towers, and all broadcast stations are plotted on *ChartGuide* charts.

In the interests of clarity, fog signals are not given here, on the assumption that you will rely more heavily on RDF. However, you will find them in the *Pacific Boating Almanac* and shown with sound characteristics on *ChartGuide* charts.

Sailing Directions are compiled from San Francisco southwards, both as a matter of editorial convenience, and because many users of this book will be heading S to Mexico. Both north- and south- bound planning strategies are included for each section of coast, and you will find the book easy to use "backwards."

The following are *not* covered in detail here:

• *San Francisco Bay* inside the Golden Gate lies outside the scope of this passage guide. We welcome you, or say farewell, as you enter or leave the entrance.

• *The offshore islands:* San Miguel, Santa Rosa, Santa Cruz, Anacapa, San Nicolas, Santa Barbara Island, Santa Catalina, and San Clemente. A detailed description of the many anchorages in the islands is hardly appropriate for a guide of this nature. You will find full information in *Cruising Guide to the Channel Islands* (Capra Press, 1979) *ChartGuide for Southern California*, (ChartGuide, Ltd. 1981-82), and in the *Pacific Boating Almanac*, (Western Marine Enterprises, 1980 and annually). Other sources are listed in chapter 2.

• *The mainland coast* between Point Piedras Blancas (N of San Simeon) and Bahia San Quintin (100 miles S of Ensenada) is covered by *ChartGuide for Southern California*, and the coast from Point Conception to Point Mugu by *Cruising Guide for the Channel Islands.*

This book tells you how to identify the harbors, gives details of the entrance channels, and a summary comment about slips and facilities.

Again, the amount of detail available is too massive for this volume. We recommend the *Pacific Boating Almanac* or *ChartGuide for Southern California (ChartGuide Ltd,* Anaheim, California, 92801) for exploring these ports: they are designed for just such a purpose and revised annually. Both these publications contain diving and fishing information, the latter in great detail. *California Coastal Passages* is cross-referenced to NOS charts, to *Southern California Chart Kit,* and to *ChartGuide for Southern California.* The latter are books of NOS charts, exact reproductions cut to small-craft size, ChartGuide being updated from Local Notices to Mariners and local sources, adding much local detail on its charts.

Disclaimer

This book has been compiled from both official and private information sources, as well as the author's practical experience of the area. Any opinions expressed here are those of the author, and not of the US Coast Guard or other government agencies. And, while every effort has been made to ensure the accuracy of this volume, neither the publishers, nor the author, can assume any responsibility for errors in charts, pilotage, sailing directions, soundings, or other information in these pages.

Sources

Research for *California Coastal Passages* involved consulting a mass of archival, historical, and navigational information. The following were basic sources:
- *US Coast Pilot 7* for 1979 and earlier editions back to 1858,
- NOS and earlier official charts dating back to 1853,
- *Chart Kit for Southern California* (Better Boating Association, Needham, Mass., 1979),
- *Local Notices to Mariners* and *Weekly Notices to Mariners,*
- Army Corps of Engineers, *Small Craft Ports and Anchorages,* 1949.
- *ChartGuide for Southern California* 1979-80 and ChartGuide for Catalina Island (ChartGuide, Ltd. Anaheim, CA 92801)

- *Pacific Boating Almanac,* Northern and Southern California editions (Western Marine Enterprises, 1980),
- Leland R. Lewis and Peter E. Ebeling, *Sea Guide, Volume One: Southern California* (Sea Publications, Newport Beach, 3rd ed. 1973),
- *Ocean Passages for the World*(Hydrographer of the Navy, 1979)
- *Admiralty Pilot* for California (Hydrographer of the Navy)1973).
- Articles in *Sea, Pacific Skipper,* and other periodicals,

Acknowledgements

- To the dozens of sailors, merchant seamen, and commercial fishing people who have consciously, or unconsciously, contributed to this volume.
- To Peter Howorth, who reviewed the manuscript in detail, provided many photographs, and invaluable information on the California weather conditions from his vast experience.
- To Earl Sweetman of Lompoc, who flew me over Point Conception and elsewhere in Central California.
- To Jim Cunningham and John Gainor for critiquing the draft manuscript.
- To Graham Pomeroy, who also read the manuscript, made many valuable suggestions, and provided many photographs.
- To Noel Young, who provided encouragement, stimulating advice, and suggested the book in the first place. And to his colleagues at Capra Press, who made production and design a joy.
- To Alyson Nethery, who drew the charts and plans for the book with great skill and sensitivity. And also to the various photographers who provided pictures for the book. They are credited individually with their pictures.
- To all those who shared the cruises that led to this book with me.

California Coastal Passages

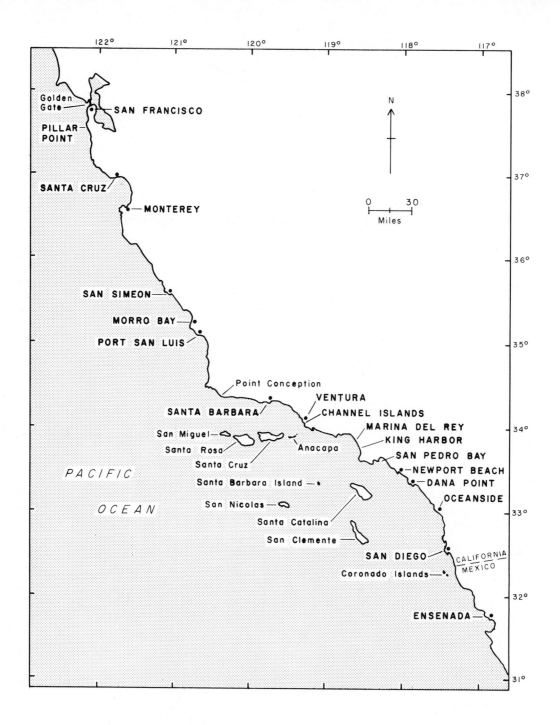

PART I

CALIFORNIA PASSAGE-MAKING

"I am convinced that vessels, with the winds we had from the bay of San Francisco to Point Conception, or indeed further to the northward, would make as good a passage with the assistance of the land winds, which in general blow from the east to the northwestward, as they would with the sea breeze to the south-eastward, since the land wind prevails during a larger proportion of the twenty-four hours than the sea breeze..."
—GEORGE VANCOUVER, *1794.*

"It has been advised to work close along shore to northern ports during the summer northwest winds, and take chances of the land breezes to make latitude, but the attempt will double the length of any voyage. Baffling light airs and calms frequently exist along the coast, while vessels several hundred miles off have strong NW winds. Moreover, we know that the current frequently sets two miles per hour from the northward. In our experience, we never yet have met with a wind off the land north of San Francisco, and very rarely, indeed, south of it, except in the region of the Santa Barbara channel."
—GEORGE DAVIDSON, *1858.*

CHAPTER 1

Passage-making: Yachts, and Equipment

There are times in the cruising life that remain in memory, year after year until the end of one's days. I am fortunate in that many of my unforgettable cruising memories come from voyages in California waters. They stand out as fresh as the day they happened. I remember feeling my way towards Morro Bay in a dense summer fog, drifting slowly under main and genoa, eyes straining into the gloom. Suddenly the fog lifted to reveal the great rock like a signpost half mile ahead. Our tension evaporated in a surge of quiet relief. The breakfast that followed will remain a legend forever.

There are other moments, too, many of them at anchor in remote coves of the offshore islands, far from the roar of freeways and the temptation of credit card restaurants. A glass of wine in hand, the soft music of the ever present surf, they combine to create a permanent magic for the soul. Cruising in California is a kaleidoscope of memories, of calms and heavy weather, of memorable yachts and unusual people, of sharp, blue days and longer passages, of special smells and leisurely conversations. We are lucky to sail in a cruising ground that has a special magic and more than its share of evocative places. I hope, this book will help you reach some of them.

Some years ago, Graham Pomeroy and I compiled a *Cruising Guide*, in which we described the many harbors and anchorages of the Santa Barbara Channel region. This book introduced me to dozens of new friends, many of whom gave suggestions for the improvement of the guide, and shared their own memories and impressions with us. I also met a considerable number of people who were uneasy about making longer passages to reach the best cruising grounds in California. "It's fine to talk about the joys of Santa Cruz Island or the Sacramento delta," they complained, "but we're apprehensive about the open water passage from Marina del Rey to the islands, or to San Francisco. What about the weather and rough seas? How do we make progress to windward? What about currents and tides offshore? Isn't Point Conception too dangerous for small yachts?" This book is designed to help you plan and execute longer passages between San Francisco and Ensenada. As such, it is somewhat of an innovation in cruising guides, most of which concentrate on harbor hopping rather than longer journeys.

PASSAGE-MAKING IN CALIFORNIA

The West Coast between San Francisco and Ensenada offers a remarkable constellation of cruising grounds, from the sheltered but windy reaches of the Bay area to remote islands and the urbanized, marina-oriented Southern California mainland. However, to reach any of these cruising grounds from another, you are bound to make a longer passage, either close along the coast, or far offshore. Such journeys can be as short as 30 miles, or as long as several hundred, most of them out of sight of land. Unless you are making a local cruise, you will have to plan at least two longer passages to and from your cruising ground. Even within a relatively homogeneous area like Southern California, there are important variables of weather, wind, and passage timing to be taken into consideration. Anyone contemplating a longer passage in California comes up against several immediate realities:

• Prevailing winds blow from N to S along the mainland coast. At least one direction of a return journey from one California harbor to another will be in face of the normal winds.

• Both foggy conditions and heavy shipping traffic can present persistent hazards for small craft at all times of the year.

• Despite claims to the contrary, California weather can be dangerously unpredictable, to the extent that survival conditions are sometimes, though rarely, encountered by the unwary.

• Cruising conditions are different N of Point Conception from those in the south.

• Considerable distances can separate refuge harbors and anchorages. Thus, a decision to divert to another port than one's destination may be impossible if the weather deteriorates. You may have to stay offshore until conditions improve.

Your preparations for an offshore passage must be made with these realities in mind, especially when selecting your yacht and the gear to equip her.

Relatively few Northern California skippers make the long passage south to the Santa Barbara Channel. Only a handful of the thousands of yachts south of Point Conception ever round this formidable headland and cruise Bay area waters. Southern California cruising people enjoy a vast sailing area with relatively pleasant weather year round. Experienced sailors can cruise in almost complete safety provided they watch the subtle signs of changing weather. On the face of it, there are few incentives to head north against the prevailing winds. North of Point Conception, these winds blow harder, the waters are cooler, and the iron-bound coast is open to the fetch of thousands of miles of open Pacific. A passage up or down the Central California coast is a different proposition from battling 30-knot winds in the sheltered Bay or crossing the Santa Barbara Channel. Anyone sailing out under the Golden Gate Bridge is faced with a full day's open water sailing even to reach Drake's Bay to the north, or Pillar Point Harbor to the south. To the novice, a passage down to Point Conception and beyond can seem as lengthy as an ocean voyage. Just the thought of rounding Point Conception puts off even experienced sailors. Bar stories about this historic promontory abound in every yacht club between Seattle and Ensenada. Point Conception's reputation is not helped by (true) tales of Transpac racers who sail to its windy vicinity to practice heavy weather sailing.

This passage guide is based on three fundamental assumptions about coastal voyaging in California, aimed at dispelling myths:

• The differences in weather and ocean conditions north and south of Point Conception are ones of degree rather than dramatic change.

• Point Conception can be rounded in complete safety, *provided* you time your passage carefully.
• Much of your cruising involves contrary winds, and your passage must be planned to accomodate them.

One problem is that few reliable sources of cruising information exist on the California coast. Our state of knowledge, in an era when official publications are designed for supertankers, is akin to that facing the windjammer skipper in the 1850s. In the absence of reliable charts, they navigated with the aid of school atlases.

Planning Your Cruise: The Ideal Yacht

While prehistoric Indians paddled regularly across to the offshore islands, they chose their weather carefully. You can see all manner of weird craft wending their way to Catalina on a summer's weekend. But no sane skipper would undertake a long passage off the California coast in anything but a well-found yacht with adequate waterline length, covered decks, and strong rigging. You can cruise among the Southern California islands in perfect safety in a well found trailer yacht, provided you wait for settled conditions. So theoretically at any rate, you should be able to take any standard 25-foot or larger, deep keel production yacht anywhere between San Francisco and Ensenada. Unfortunately, however, many well-known designs manufactured in California are rigged too lightly for anything but average Southern California conditions, where the winds rarely blow stronger than 25 knots. Many southern yachts have extra high rigs to compensate for prevailing light conditions, while Bay area sailors add heavy-duty stays, and sometimes even stronger mast sections. The first criterion for any offshore yacht is that she be strong enough to ride out a severe gale at sea.

The immediate reaction of many people to an offshore passage is to choose as heavy a displacement a yacht as possible. California marinas are crowded with massive, "traditional" heavy displacement boats that look gorgeous but sail to windward like the proverbial cow. They are unable to make progress against even wind waves, and end up motor sailing for long dreary hours while their lighter brethren enjoy a smooth and rapid passage upwind. The objective of any offshore passage is to get to one's destination as soon as possible. The process of getting there may be enjoyable, but it is far more fun if you cover the ground as fast as possible. Then consider the fatigue factor. A night in port gained by a fast passage is far preferable to an extra period of darkness in the open sea. California offshore conditions include a high proportion of light air days. A moderate to light displacement yacht with good light air performance, and superior windward abilities makes the best cruising boat for our offshore conditions. A decade ago, the offshore sailor wanting performance was condemned to a narrow, uncomfortable vessel with minimal accomodation that sailed on her ear. Today, you can choose from a wide range of supremely comfortable offshore yachts that sail as well as their racing ancestors.

When choosing a vessel for offshore passage-making in California, you should select one with the following features:

• Adequate waterline and overall length to handle ocean swells and wind waves up to 10 feet or more, and winds of up to 75 knots in an emergency.

• Moderate to light displacement with fin, or modified fin keel hull design, with superior windward performance and good tracking ability downwind. Beware of some well-known racing designs that have a reputation for squirrelly performance downwind. Hull construction must be superior quality.

• A rig of adequate strength to survive full gale conditions at sea and repeated knockdowns in severe conditions. I have a strong bias towards a single mast rig, on the grounds that it is far simpler to operate shorthanded. Most California production boats have masthead sloop rigs, but a cutter configuration is ideal for offshore work where frequent sail changes are needed. A roller furling jib is a useful feature, but you should be able to set a storm jib if need be.

• A diesel engine of sufficient power to move the yacht to windward against a bumpy swell at 5 to 6 knots. Outboard engines have no place on my ideal offshore boat.

• Comfortable *passage* berths for an offshore crew, sufficient for each member of the crew to have a bunk to themselves. These bunks should be fitted with detachable leeboards. A passage berth is quite different from what may be an ideal bunk in port. You should be able to jam yourself into it with comfort when going to windward in a rough sea. Many production yachts that claim to sleep six in fact offer about two passage berths, if that.

• Gimbelled cooking facilities that can be used even under the severe conditions.

• Adequate navigation space, including a strong chart table.

• The minimum number of through hull fittings, and these of the highest quality.

• The interior should be designed for passage-making rather than marina living, include a permanently secured chart table and adequate handholds below, and enjoy superior ventilation.

• The decks must be protected with fore and aft pulpits and over-strength double lifelines.

• Navigation lights that conform to Coast Guard and international rules of the road.

Above all, choose a vessel that fits both your pocket book and your family needs. We all have our biasses. You may be a purist who refuses to ship aboard with an engine and fervently believes in heavy displacement yachts. That is your privilege and choice, provided you do not compromise on safety and strength. One of the pleasures of cruising is watching your tastes in suitable designs change over the years.

Planning Your Cruise: Safety Gear

Anyone sailing offshore in California should plan to be as completely equipped with safety gear as possible. Assume that you will meet rough weather one day, and that you may have to fend for yourself for a considerable time before help arrives. Coast Guard and offshore racing requirements are minimal yardsticks for serious cruising. You should carry:

• Adequate ground tackle including two anchors of sufficient weight to hold you in relatively exposed anchorages during a full gale.

- Life packets of USCG approved design for every member of the crew, equipped with lights and whistles.
- A "Transpac" pole, U-shaped life ring, Xenon overboard light, drogue, and die canister, all mounted on the stern pulpit.
- Deck safety harnesses for all members of the crew.
- A radar reflector, preferably mounted permanently.
- A set of day and night flares in excess of USCG requirements.
- At least 2 bilge pumps, one mounted in the cabin, the second operable from the cockpit. Some people install an automatic bilge pump, which is a useful precaution, provided you watch your batteries.
- A minimum of 2 fire extinguishers, one near the engine room and galley, the other readily accessible in the cockpit.
- A Freon horn and a backup manual foghorn.
- A permanently mounted compass, *swung for deviation.* Make sure you have a bearing compass aboard as a back-up. Each compass should be adequately lit.
- Wooden plugs for emergency repairs for through-hull fittings.
- A sharp knife and a pair of heavy duty bolt cutters for clearing away after a dismasting. Having had a yacht dismasted, I am a firm believer in adequately stayed deck-stepped masts.
- A VHF radio with channel 16, the emergency frequency.
- An Emergency Locator Beacon, mounted near the cockpit. Remember to check the batteries of this, and other battery-operated equipment, regularly.
- A waterproof first aid kit, with supplies to cover fractures, and other shipboard accidents.
- Last, but by no means least, an inflatable liferaft adequate to accommodate all members of the crew in the event you have to abandon ship. This requires annual servicing. No serious offshore sailor should be without one. Nearly every cruising yacht in European waters carries a liferaft as a matter of course. Since California sailing conditions can be just as severe, it is surprising more people do not routinely carry one. The soft canister type is probably best, for it can be stowed below when you are in harbor, a precaution that protects it from heat and moisture and extends its life. The liferaft must be mounted close to the cockpit, with the release line near at hand. The survival kit

with the raft will probably suffice for coastal passages, but you may care to add a hold-all filled with essential items for yourself, a bag which is ready to go, and stowed within close reach of the helm.

Safety gear for offshore cruising is expensive, but it is a false economy not to use the best. Do not fall into the syndrome that "it will never happen to me."

Planning Your Cruise: Cruising Gear

Having the right equipment aboard makes all the difference for a comfortable offshore passage. Unfortunately, most of us tend to equip our yachts with all kinds of elaborate and unnecessary gear. Treat electronic gear as something which is useful, yet equipment that you do not have to depend upon. My advice is to keep it simple and avoid as much electrical gear as you can. Here are some essential items:

• A sound dinghy is an expensive but essential priority. A good inflatable is useful for California conditions where you tend to land on rocks as well as sandy beaches. Avons and Zodiacs are commonplace, but costly. Shop around for a good domestically built inflatable. There are now a few on the market. Your inflatable should be equipped with good oars and rowlocks, adequate safety buoyancy, a bailer, and strong tow lines. A repair kit is essential. Make sure you can row your inflatable against a strong wind. Your outboard may fail. A word of warning: do not try to tow an inflatable at sea. They have an alarming tendency to fly aboard in strong following winds.

Many owners of larger yachts prefer a fiberglass or wooden dinghy to stow aboard. A hard dinghy makes all the difference on a long trip, but takes up valuable stowage space on a relatively short California cruise. Unless you enjoy dinghy sailing and exploring shallow creeks, it is probably better to rely on an inflatable. Do not be tempted to tow a hard dinghy astern, for you will be faced with a swamped tender in anything but the calmest conditions. Personally, I regard stern davits as an abomination, but many people like them. I find everything in creation gets tangled up with them, and they are vulnerable in heavy weather.

• A good boarding ladder is an essential. If possible, invest in one that hinges down over the stern. You then have a permanent ladder for use in emergencies.

• Electronics make life easier, but you can cruise comfortably without them. An accurate log and depth sounder are invaluable for Dead Reckoning navigation and essential during foggy conditions and at night. A good RDF set makes offshore navigation much more re-assuring. Expensive devices like Loran and satellite navigators are not strictly necessary, although useful crew members. You are unlikely to need celestial navigation to sail between San Francisco and Ensenada.

• Good fenders and mooring lines, as well as adequate springs, will help you sleep at night in strange harbors. Carry plenty of small stuff, rags, and short lengths for emergencies and chafing gear.

• A good tool kit and an adequate spares inventory make good sense. Your tool kit should include wrenches to fit every nut on the boat, including the stuffing box. Any good primer on cruising will provide you with a check list. Commonly used spares are engine belts, water pump impellors, motor oil, shackles, winch parts, spare turnbuckles and rope, batteries, fuses for key electrical equipment, repair manuals, fiberglass repair kits, stove parts, batteries, and extra winch handles. Again, be guided by your own experience and that of others. It is pointless, for example, to carry a new starter motor in our well traveled waters when you can always sail to a nearby port within a couple of days. Make sure you carry plenty of spare halliards, as well as a reserve of fresh water and fuel.

• Your galley equipment will need little modification for offshore passages in California. We use lots of bag and seals to carry large, precooked casseroles aboard. A supply of large plastic garbage bags makes life easier, for no responsible skipper allows garbage to be dumped over the side.

• A cockpit awning makes sense on hot summer days, but Bimini covers are unnecessary in our relatively cool climate.

• Self steering vanes are becoming more commonplace on coastal cruising boats, but I would be inclined not to invest in one. Most of your sailing takes place in ship- and fishing boat-infested waters, where a good lookout is vital. In any case, few of your passages will last longer than 4 or 5 days. The money spent on a vane is better spent on a liferaft or some other essential. If you do decide to fit one, be sure to talk to people who own them first, preferably someone with a yacht like yours.

Your gear inventory can expand to include every form of luxury, from refrigerators to flopper-stoppers. My counsel is to keep it simple, and enjoy sailing rather than maintenance. Make sure, however, that your registration papers, radio log and license, and insurance policy are aboard, even if sailing in local waters. Many owners maintain a yacht log as well, a useful record in case of an insurance claim, and great fun to read on winter's evenings as well.

Planning Your Cruise: Personal Gear

California is far from a tropical marine environment, so your crew should be instructed to bring warm clothing. For offshore passage-making, insist that everyone bring adequate waterproof clothing, and *inspect it ahead of time.* Many people buy flotation coats, sometimes with safety harnesses built into them. Woollen watch caps are desirable for night sailing, while you should insist that everyone wear non-skid deck shoes. If you plan a voyage north of Point Conception, every member of the crew should acquire waterproof sailing boots. The lightweight French and Scandinavian designs are a good choice. Sunglasses make both watchkeeping and navigation much easier. So do wide-brimmed sun hats with chin straps. Every crew member should bring their own knives, spikes, and safety harnesses, and be told to pack everything in a canvas hold-all. Suitcases should not go aboard.

Once everything is assembled and before you provision the yacht, make sure you and your crew know where every piece of gear on the boat is stowed. Can you, dear reader, locate your bolt cutters within 15 seconds on a dark and rainy night with Point Conception a mile to leeward? If you can, chances are you will enjoy thousands of miles of worry free passage-making.

CHAPTER 2

Passage Planning: Natural Hazards

The art of successful passage-making in California can be summarized in two words: careful planning. Any return voyage along the coast, for example, must be predicated on the assumption that you will be traveling against the prevailing winds either outward or homeward bound. You must allow the extra time to do so. A successful passage from the mainland to the offshore islands of the south is dependent not on weather conditions inshore, but on island weather that should be tracked carefully several days ahead. If ever there was a cruising area where advance planning was important, this is it.

SOURCES OF PLANNING INFORMATION

Every passage-making yacht should have a complete set of NOS charts for her chosen cruising area on board. These should include not only the passage charts where courses are laid off and DR plots maintained, but large scale charts of harbors, islands, and other hazards. You can voyage from San Francisco to Ensenada using about 6 passage charts; indeed I once met a 35-footer sailing from San Francisco to Los Angeles with only a road map on board. The careful skipper ensures that adequate coverage is aboard. I learned this the hard way, when bound from Falmouth, England, to Ribadeo in Northern Spain. One hundred miles off the coast an unexpected northerly gale blew up, making Ribadeo a lee shore. We decided to make for the all-weather harbor at Bayona, on the West Coast. Since I had no large scale chart of this unfamiliar haven aboard, we were forced to remain hove-to 20 miles offshore in a shipping lane until the gale moderated. I won't make that mistake again.

One useful way to acquire a complete folio of Southern California NOS and DMAHC charts, at a fraction of the cost of separate charts, is to purchase either *Southern California Chart Kit* (Better Boating Association, P. O. Box 407, Needham, Mass. 02192) or *ChartGuide for Southern California* (from marine supply stores or ChartGuide Ltd., 300 No. Wilshire #5, Anaheim, CA 92801). Both books have pre-plotted courselines with magnetic bearings. So popular are these that I have cross-referenced them in this book.

Chart Kit is a spiral-bound book of charts cut to 17" x 22", and most convenient for actual plotting, covering Point Conception to Ensenada without Coast Pilot 7 or local data. *ChartGuide* is a book opening to 14" x 20" charts covering from San Simeon to Bahia San Quintin with enlargements, aerial photos, special charts not available from NOS, Coast Pilot 7 extracts, local information, and roses for plotting special courses.

Individual NOS and DMAHC charts can be obtained from a helpful chart agent in Oxnard: Pacific Compass and Navigation Company. 3201 S Victoria Avenue, Oxnard, CA 93030. (805) 985-2364.

The small boat owner is not well served by official sailing directions. You were taken care of a century ago, when small sailing vessels plied the coast and made use of anchorages that few commercial ships use today. George Davidson's *Coast Pilot* was first published in 1858 and remains a mine of information for yacht owners. I have included some of his finest sailing directions here. The *US Coast Pilot* no. 7, which covers California, is issued annually. It is designed for large commercial vessels, but contains valuable information if you are prepared to dig for it. *Reed's Nautical Almanac*, West Coast edition, contains invaluable navigational tables.

By far the best information source on a day-to-day basis is the *Pacific Boating Almanac,* published by Western Marine Enterprises, Box Q, Ventura, CA 93001. The *Almanac* appears annually, in three editions: Southern California, Arizona and Baja Northern California and Nevada; and the Pacific Northwest. This is an information publication, partially subsidized by advertising. The data it contains is accurate, up-to-date, and compiled by people who know what they are talking about. This is your source on facilities, lights and radio frequencies, tide tables, and other cruising information that needs annual updating. Although the *Almanac* includes some sailing directions and lengthy extracts from official publications,it can hardly be classified as a cruising guide. Nevertheless, no serious California sailor should be without an up-to-date edition.

The Bay area has no cruising guide, but Southern California and the offshore islands are served by Leland Lewis and Peter Ebeling's *Sea Guide, Volume I - Southern California,* Sea Publications, 2nd ed., 1973. This is a "coffee table" publication with superb aerial photographs. *Cruising Guide to the Channel Islands,* (Capra Press 1979), covers the offshore islands and mainland ports between Point Arguello and Point Mugu. Both publications are available through marine bookstores.

In an unashamed plug, I recommend the Island Hunter Bookstore, 1198 Navigator Drive, Ventura, CA 93003, (805) 644-5827, as a source of all marine publications. Karin Jensen will gladly order the most esoteric publications for you, will supply by mail, and issues a regular catalog. Her tiny store is a nautical book collector's delight.

NATURAL CRUISING HAZARDS

The potential hazards of California passage-making can be divided into two major groups: weather related dangers like winds, waves, and fogs, and humanly caused perils such as shipping, navigational regulations, missile ranges, oil rigs, and floating debris like crates or drums. Your planning strategies should take as many of these variables into account as possible.

WEATHER CONDITIONS

Fortunately for small boat owners, coastal weather conditions in Central and Southern California are usually fairly stable. Southern California sailors cruise all the year round, while many northerners either restrict their activities to the Bay or effectively lay up their boats during the winter. Weather conditions on the California coast are radically affected by high and low pressure systems offshore and in the interior. Major shifts in the weather are relatively predictable. Nevertheless, local conditions may differ drastically from a general situation prevailing over, say, Northern California. The key to successful weather forecasting is not only to monitor weather maps in the newspapers and on TV, and to track VHF channels WX-1 and WX-2, but to learn the subtle signs that nature gives us for impending weather changes. The statements about California weather which follow are a generalized summary and assume that you have access to the WX channels as they plot changing meterological conditions.

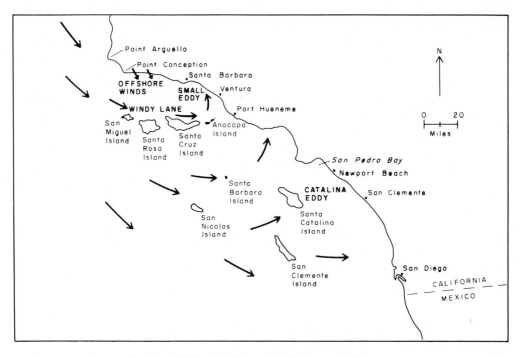

Catalina Eddy conditions in Southern California.

Summer Weather

The so-called North Pacific High dominates the weather map off the California coast during the summer months. This creates a common condition where a long-lived high pressure system sits off the California coast, while low pressure sits in the interior. These conditions create a pressure differential that maintains an air flow in from the Pacific over the coast. As this air passes over the cool waters of the coast, a relatively cool layer, often called the "marine layer," is formed. The pressure gradient between the high and low zones dominates weather patterns over the coast and creates a prevailing NW air stream parallel to most of the California coast. This wind blows almost parallel to the coast until it reaches Point Arguello, where the shoreline turns east. A wind of between 25 and 35 knots now fans out both offshore toward San Nicolas Island and inshore along the east-west mainland coast.

When the wind blows from NW at 15 knots or more along the outer Channel Islands, it slows as it fans towards shore, sometimes changing direction. The NW wind backs to W past San Nicolas Island, then SW as it approaches Catalina. The eddy is formed when the breeze approaches the shore, loses strength, then comes out of the S and SE. By this time it has reversed its original direction, forming the characteristic eddy. The Catalina Eddy is often accompanied by fog and low clouds at the coast. If San Nicolas reports clear skies and NW winds over 15 knots, the Eddy is probably in effect.

The marine layer contrasts sharply with the warmer air that lies at higher altitudes over the coast. The transition zone between the marine layer and the warmer air above it is known as the "inversion layer." The intensity of this inversion layer depends on temperature differences between the cold and warm air. It serves as a lid which suppresses vertical air movement. Cooler air tends to stay in the layer, bacause it is too dense to rise into warmer zones. The dense fog and low, stratus clouds so familiar to California sailors tend to form under these conditions.

One type of California fog is formed by warm, moist sea air blowing inshore and striking cold water near the coast. The air condenses, forming a thick fog bank. The cold water has been drawn to surface by offshore winds that disperse warmer water seaward. Such offshore winds are frequent between Gaviota and Point Arguello, where cold upwelling and warm Pacific winds form fog banks that can lie close offshore for weeks. When the wind subsides, the fog drifts inshore over the coast. Sea, or advection, fog like this is common between May and July and is prevalent N of Santa Monica.

Radiation fog is formed as the land radiates heat after sundown. The warm air rises, drawing in colder air just above the ground. The air cools, condenses, and forms a fog bank that usually burns off by mid-morning. Radiation fogs are most common S of Long Beach between September and January.

Coastal fog and low clouds tend to be thickest during the night and morning hours. As the air near the land surface warms up during the day, lower air layers reach a temperature similar to the air above the inversion and the fog dissipates into hazy afternoon sunshine. Both land and sea fogs vanish when a strong wind gets up, tend to form during calm weather. An alert skipper can sometimes find stronger wind on the edge of a fog bank.

During summer months, the North Pacific High strengthens and migrates northward, with its eastern edge off the coast of Oregon and California. Cold water that flows southward along the coast maintains cooler temperatures anp assists in chilling the overlying air and causing the inversion. This results in stable weather conditions along the coast. Low pressure systems that pass across the Pacific are diverted N far away from California. May, June, and July are usually the foggiest months from Ventura northwards. Thick, grey overcast days can persist for days, even weeks. Such conditions reduce visibility at sea but are often the best weather for making passages to windward. In other words, a yacht wanting to cruise to San Francisco may have excellent conditions for the passage between May and July. If a thermally induced low pressure center is created in south western Arizona, then the sea breeze tends to strengthen along the coast during the afternoons, increasing the strength of the prevailing NW winds. This can cause strong headwinds N of Point Conception, and less favorable passage conditions.

California summer weather tends to be foggy from May through mid-July, with muggy, hot conditions prevailing from mid-July to the middle of September. Hot, dry days are more common from then until October, or even November. September to November, even December or January, are the seasons when dry, hot NE winds can blow. The most notorious is the NE "Santa Ana" wind condition that can cause havoc S of Point Conception. Santa Anas sweep into Southern California when higher pressures fill in over Nevada and Utah. Such conditions often occur in fall and winter when a front has moved inland through Northern California and is followed by a high pressure build up over the Pacific Northwest and the Great Basin. A steep pressure gradient brings the winds over the mountains down into Southern California. As they spill over the summits, the winds are heated by downslope compression at the rate of about 5.5 degrees F./thousand feet. If the descending, heated air is cooler than the air

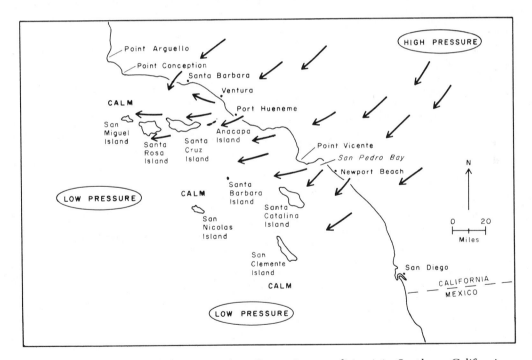

Wind patterns in severe NE weather (Santa Ana conditions) in Southern California.

over the coastal plain, it will push the cool marine air out to sea and sweep over the entire coastal plain with great velocity. These "cold" Santa Anas are far more dangerous than the so-called "warm" versions of the same condition, which tend to be more localized.

Strong, onshore NW winds can sometimes bring cool sea air into land basins near the coast. When the NW breeze drops, the trapped air heated by the land sweeps out of the basins down the coastal

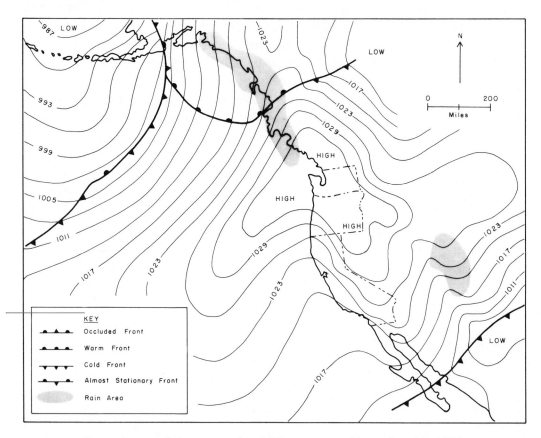

Santa Ana conditions over the California coast. November 19, 1956.

canyons. Such winds are sometimes called "Sundowners," since they are most common at dusk.

Santa Ana conditions can last three or four days, with the strongest winds blowing in the first couple of days. They can be dangerous for small craft, especially when encountered at the mouth of large coastal canyons.

N of Point Conception, you will encounter down-canyon winds during prevailing NW conditions. These blow at dawn and dusk and can reach dangerous velocities locally. I was once knocked on my beam ends in a heavy displacement 30-footer off Conception by a sudden downslope gust. Luckily, we had a reef in the main and a smaller genoa set just in case of such squalls. If possible avoid passage-making in Santa Ana and offshore conditions. The weather will be hot, dry, and crystal clear. But the winds will be dangerously unpredictable for inexperienced sailors. A sure sign of impending down slope winds: very dry, still conditions associated with a slight swell from NE. If berthed in an exposed anchorage under such conditions, be prepared to leave at very short notice. You may find yourself anchored on a lee shore in gale force winds, as dozens of yachts did at Santa Cruz Island over Thanksgiving, 1977.

Occasionally, maritime tropical air invades Baja and Southern California, bringing hot, humid weather and thunderstorms to the coast. The winds are light and sailing tends to be unpleasant. Extremely rare tropical storms have been recorded in Southern California, in which case you should be snug in port. Even distant Mexican storms can generate 6 to 8-foot swells that radiate from storm centers hundreds of miles away. These can arrive in S-facing anchorages without warning in sets of half a dozen or more swells that could throw you up on the beach. Your best guard against these "sneakers" is to monitor the VHF weather channels that track the course of tropical storms off Baja. Heavy, sudsy foam close inshore can be a sign of heavy surge, and you should monitor S-facing beaches carefully for this condition when tropical storms are reported, usually between June and early October.

Winter Weather

Winter weather is still dominated by the position of the North Pacific High, but the high pressure weakens and migrates to the south. Thus, fog and low clouds are still common during periods of dry, stable weather. The weakening and southern movement of the anticyclone allows large Pacific storms to approach the coast. Many more such low pressure systems pass through Northern California than the south. Fortunately for the small boat sailor, such storms are usually carefully

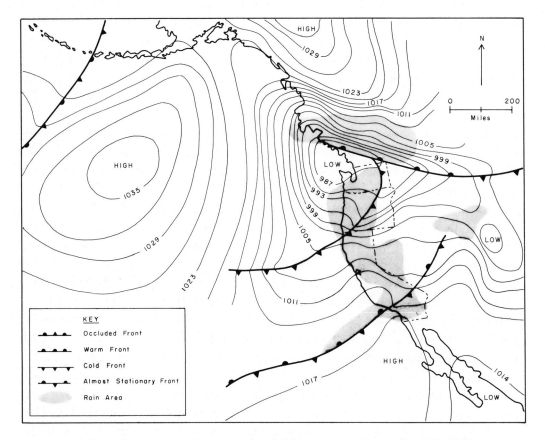

A frontal system passing over the California coast. December 29, 1964.

tracked by the National Weather Service long before they reach the coast. The circulation of air around the low center is such that the leading edges, or "fronts," are formed between warm and cold air masses. Clouds, shifting winds, and rain develop along these fronts, caused by mixing and turbulence.

Southeasters seldom strike without warning and are tracked by satellites far offshore. As the storm approaches, prevailing westerlies die out and dark cumulus clouds gather. The water close inshore is usually turbid, but now begins to clear. The clouds appear to settle, squalls occur, followed by steady rain. After several hours, the SE wind decreases. As the storm passes, skies begin to clear and the wind shifts to NW or W, depending on your location. If you intend a passage during a period of stormy weather, watch the direction from which the lows arrive:

• Lows from the NW come from the Gulf of Alaska. They bring unstable, cool air with them. The SE winds associated with the system will gradually veer round to W as the rain and gusty winds pass through. As the skies clear, the winds can blow up to 50 knots. Avoid passage-making under these conditions if humanly possible. *Above all, do not be tempted to ride the SE condition northbound unless a safe port is close at hand. You will encounter gale force headwinds within a few hours.* If you must sail, radio ahead for a weather check at your destination first.

• Lows from the W are often associated with a broad area of low pressure extending over the latitudes of the east Pacific. Such conditions can bring a whole string of rain-filled storm systems to Northern California. The entire state enjoys a relatively prolonged period of wet and stormy weather. Your chances of having some longer periods of SE wind are somewhat improved under these circumstances, but do not be tempted to take on a longer passage.

• The heaviest rainfall often comes from lows that approach from SW. Massive cloud banks preceed the storm, the winds shift to SE, and then to WNW as the storm clears relatively slowly compared with NW lows. Temperatures remain more constant. You may have more warning both of approaching SE conditions and of post-frontal winds with SE lows.

The greatest danger with low pressure systems lies in the unstable, blustery conditions that can develop after they have moved on. Violent squalls, heavy rain showers, even waterspouts are not uncommon.

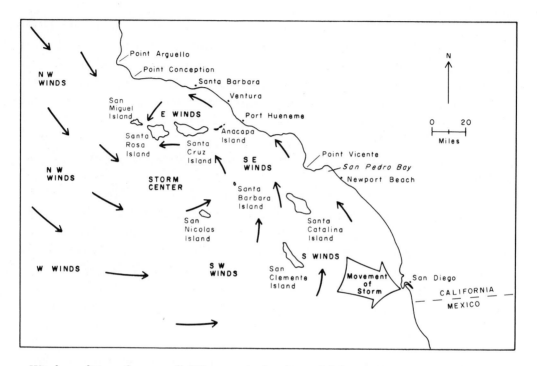

Wind conditions for a small SE storm in Southern California. E, SE, and S winds bring rain; SW, W, and NW winds bring rapidly clearing skies. Note how the winds bend around the land masses.

Southeasters become less common by April. Gusty NW gales now pose a dangerous hazard, especially in Central and Northern California. This onshore flow of moist air displaces rising warmer air over the land. Then night falls and the land cools to nearly the same temperature as the ocean. The wind drops close inshore. Moist air condenses on coastal mountain ranges where the air is coldest, especially near the low passes. Once the air temperature is cooler than the water, winds begin to blow offshore, usually until early morning.

Veil clouds on the mountains are scattered as land temperatures again rise. By noon the next day, the onshore wind fills in again, to repeat the same cycle.

Veil clouds near Point Conception

Photo: PETER HOWORTH

Veil clouds, or cloud caps, are valuable indicators of NW conditions. They are easily recognized: white, solid-looking clouds that cling to mountain passes and ridges, and to the W end of the offshore islands. At dawn or dusk, veil clouds may resemble an enormous wave breaking over the mountains. As the wind picks up and the land warms, the huge cloud breaks up into spinning "cotton balls," sometimes called "puff clouds." The clouds usually disappear by late morning and reappear after sundown. Here are some pointers on northwesters and veil clouds:

• The extent of the clouds is determined by the amount of wind that formed them in the first place.
• The more clouds present in the early morning, the stronger the wind will be.

• If other clouds are present as well, the northwester will last only a few hours.

• If the other clouds disappear and the veil clouds remain, plan on a three to five-day gale. These longer blows are commonest in the spring months.

• Severe Northwesters often strike the northern coastline before the south. Listen to weather reports from Point Pinos and and Piedras Blancas on the Big Sur coast. Point Arguello and San Nicolas Island reporting stations also lie in the direct path of the strongest northwesterlies, and provide a valuable check on cloud indicators.

Weather Signs

Weather signs like veil clouds are often more reliable than the taped weather forecasts so beloved by radio disc jockeys. Southern California's *"Point Conception to the Mexican border, winds light and variable morning hours, westerlies 10-18 knots in the afternoon"* is a local joke. You can combine the monitoring of VHF WX-1 and WX-2 with subtle natural signs you can learn by constant experience. Here are some passage-making pointers:

• You will probably encounter settled, and predictable, weather conditions when fog and low clouds persist nights and mornings. To make sure, keep a check on the position of the North Pacific High on your local newspaper or TV station weather map. Dewy conditions are often a sign of settled weather.

• Good visibility, hard grey profiles of distant land formations, and constantly changing, grey cloud banks may indicate an approaching frontal system. It is inadvisable to make your departure until conditions settle down.

• Clear skies, brilliantly crystal visibility, and billowing white clouds streaming from mountain tops and island summits offshore are probable signs of strong winds. Veil clouds are reliable indicators of strong NW winds.

• Clear, cool weather with snow on the mountains can mean cold, unstable conditions offshore.

• Cumulo-nimbus clouds over the mountains or turbulent clouds in the same area: summer showers and squalls from SW are likely.

• Hot, dry, and very clear conditions, with dry decks and a NE swell with no wind are clear signs of an offshore wind condition. So are layers of smog blown offshore from the Bay cities or Los Angeles. Probable unpredictable cruising conditions.

A barometer is a useful piece of equipment if you plan to be at sea during unstable winter conditions. Most small boat sailors lack the sophisticated equipment that enables professional weather forecasters to track high pressure systems and storm fronts. But you can work wonders of forecasting by relying on your own observations.

WINDS, WAVES, AND FOG

California passage-making weather is normally moderate, with prolonged periods of calm weather. Unless you are a total purist or own an ultra light displacement yacht, you should reconcile yourself to long periods of motoring in night and early morning hours. These calm periods are of great importance to someone planning a cruise to windward, as are the predictable afternoon westerlies that affect the timing of your passages in the southerly direction or out to the offshore islands. The strongest coastal winds, beyond Santa Anas, are likely to be W to NW conditions that can blow as strong as 50 to 60 knots after the passage of a frontal system. These are normally encountered between late September and May. While it is normally possible to remain at sea S of Point Conception, where the winds seldom exceed 45 knots, a passage, even downwind, in the northern parts of our cruising area would be extremely foolhardy. Northwesterlies seldom blow for more than two or three days, and are often followed by a calm period when passage-making is possible.

SE winds associated with winter storms normally come up after dark, often in the small hours, then strengthen the next morning. They can reach velocities of 35 to 60 knots in major storms. Sailing under such conditions, even south of Point Conception, can be dangerous. Most of the coast, including the securest ports, will be a lee shore. The best strategy is to plan your longer passages for settled westerly conditions.

Even in settled weather, local winds can create problems. Down canyon winds are a constant hazard on clear, dry days. Look out for such conditions when the radio speaks of "local gusty winds below co-astal canyons." Afternoon winds funnel through the Golden Gate with great velocity. Points Sur and Conception have a reputation for strong local winds. Anyone crossing to the offshore islands of the south must beware of "Windy Lane," a zone of stronger wind that blows down the inshore side of the major islands. Wind speeds can double in a few minutes, making reefs essential. As we shall see, some of the more benign local wind conditions can be used to your advantage when passage-making.

Anyone passage-making in California is going to spend days on end exposed to the full drift of the westerly swells of the open Pacific. Despite exaggerated tales to the contrary, 15-to 20-foot swells are unusual by California standards. Most sailors will never meet a swell higher than 6 to 8 feet, and then only in heavy weather. Regular ocean swells are nearly always with us, even on calm days. Sometimes, swell warnings are issued when heavy conditions generated by a storm far offshore reach the coast. Beware of passage-making under these conditions, for you may be unable to make progress against the waves. Islands and headlands like Arguello or Conception refract the ocean swell and cause locally confused seas that can be hazardous.

Wind waves are imposed on top of the prevailing swells by rising breezes. Some of the steepest seas may be encountered in places like "Windy Lane" where rapidly increasing afternoon winds can impose a 2- or 3-foot wind wave on top of a 4-foot swell in a few hours. Sometimes wind waves will fill in at an oblique angle to the prevailing swell, and make you very uncomfortable. Wind against current and tide conditions in a narrow defile like the Golden Gate can be hazardous, while the Potato Patch off San Francisco is notorious for its breaking seas and bumpy conditions even in moderate weather. Fortunately, the regular swell is normally a negligible hazard. Your cruise plan should try to avoid areas where confused seas are known to be commonplace. Pay close attention to swell conditions in the marine weather forecasts. They may affect not only your passage plans, but your intended anchorages as well.

Fog and low clouds are a persistent hazard in California waters, especially if you confine your passage-making to settled weather. One becomes so familiar with them that one tends to become casual about reduced visibility and relax one's vigilance. While it is true that the stratus clouds often lie about 300 feet above sea level and you can see at least half a mile, there are occasions when the fog reaches the surface, creating zero visibility. Passage-making under reduced visibility is fine, *provided* you lay off a compass course to your destination, maintain an accurate DR plot, and keep a good lookout. Be careful in planning a passage along or across shipping lanes. Big ships navigate on radar, and maintain full speed even in a fog. So do many commercial fishing boats. Hoist a radar reflector and have a foghorn handy. Your landfalls are likely to be about a half mile offshore in these conditions. A perceptible darkening of the grey will betray the presence of land, or a white flash betray surf breaking at the foot of a cliff. Watch for kelp beds and changing water colors as well. Approach the land with extreme caution in reduced visibility. Use your depth sounder to locate the 5- and 10- fathom lines, and be prepared to anchor off if you are unable to locate your position accurately. It is under these conditions that an RDF or Loran C is invaluable, enabling you to home in on a major landmark from a long distance off.

To make a passage in conditions of near-zero visibility is foolhardy. Under such circumstances, postpone your trip, or if caught out, sound the legal fog signals and keep a sharp lookout. Inshore, it is best to anchor in shallow water out of shipping lanes, sounding the bell signal required by law. Beware of fog banks that lie close offshore and roll in without warning. This condition is common at the Golden Gate, in Monterey Bay, and off Southern California. There have been occasions when I have had to set a compass course to locate Santa Barbara breakwater when only a few hundred yards outside the entrance.

CURRENTS AND TIDES

With the notable exception of San Francisco Bay and the Golden Gate, the tidal streams you are likely to encounter are generally weak and have little effect on passage-making. The general movement of tides off the California coast is SE to NW. High tide takes about 30 minutes to travel from San Diego to Point Conception. Average tidal range varies from 4 feet at the Golden Gate to 3.6 feet at Ensenada, but can reach 7 feet. Local tidal information and differences are given port by port in the sailing directions that follow.

The currents that run off California are still imperfectly understood. Sometimes an unexpected current set will affect your passage-making and set you a few miles off course. Such sets are almost impossible to predict. Your best strategy is to watch for signs of current running past buoys and isolated rocks, shaping your course accordingly. Here are the major currents that might affect your passages:

• The California Current flows southwards within 25 to 100 miles of the coast as far as Conception, then turns up to 150 miles offshore, away from the Southern California bight. It flows stronger in summer than in winter, but attains negligable speeds from the small craft's point of view. This same current swings east towards the coast near Ensenada. Part of this water turns northeast inshore and forms

• A counter current between the coast and the California current. This becomes the celebrated Davidson current north of Conception. These counter streams are best developed in the winter months.

• Coastal currents are affected by surface winds. There are onshore sets in many areas, rotary currents off the southern islands. Inshore currents flow faster in summer, and correspond with stronger sea breezes; S to SE currents are most common during this season. Winter inshore currents are less predictable.

• Local currents occur in many places. We attempt to identify these phenomena where they are recorded.

Dealing with California's weak currents and tidal streams is a matter of experience and keeping a close watch on your fixed position in areas like Point Mugu where they are known to flow more strongly. Be especially careful off Point Conception and San Miguel islands. The numerous shipwrecks in these vicinities are eloquent testimony to unpredictable currents and thick weather.

The natural hazards that face California sailors are no more formidable than those encountered in other areas. Provided you monitor the weather, and keep an accurate DR position, you should enjoy safe passages.

CHAPTER 3

Human Hazards and Planning Strategies

Our cruising ground has every delight to offer the sailor, from remote anchorages to vast, urban marinas. It is possible to spend weeks on end without seeing an automobile or a high rise building. Or you can spend every night dining in a different yacht club. But humanity's impact on the California coastal and marine environment increases every year, bringing new and unexpected perils to the small boat sailor. Any longer passage in California waters is going to be affected by one or the other of these potential perils. It is well to consider them in advance of your departure.

SHIPPING

There is something impressively majestic about a tanker or a container ship steaming along our coasts. The swells that cause you to roll around barely affect the inexorable progress of the merchant vessel. Strong northwesterlies are brushed aside in a cloud of smoke that drifts far down to leeward of the vanishing ship. These same juggernauts are far from majestic when viewed from close quarters. In fact they are downright dangerous. The number of yachts run down by large ships increases every year, and lives are lost because someone did not keep a good lookout. Shipping is a serious peril for California sailors. Commercial maritime traffic is heavy all year round. Some areas, like the Golden Gate to the Farallons, the Santa Barbara Channel, and San Pedro Bay, are slashed by purple zones on your charts. These are Traffic Separation Zones, established to lay out direction lanes for the hundreds of ships that journey to western ports. You should shape your courses to avoid these zones as much as possible. If you must cross them, do so by the quickest route, or at right angles, *giving way to any ships converging on you.* If you are running in the same direction as a traffic lane, lay off a course that keeps you well outside the shipping line. On no account sail between the lanes. This is especially important off the entrance to the Golden Gate.

The best protection against ships is to avoid them, and alter course rather than insisting on your rights. If the larger vessel does change direction, maintain your course and speed. Make sure you signal your intentions clearly, using the prescribed horn signals. Hoist a large radar reflector in reduced weather and make sure you are thoroughly familiar with the International Rules for the Prevention of Collision at Sea. Above all, give way to large ships in restricted waters where they have no space to get out of your way.

When on passage, brief your crew about the dangers of shipping, insist on a 24-hour and 360-degree lookout. Teach your crew to identify the angle of ships' lights, and how to take bearings to establish collision courses. Insist that they call the skipper if they have the slightest doubt about an approaching vessel. Display the correct navigation lights at night. Never engage a wind vane or autopilot or forget to keep a lookout. Above all, obey two basic rules:

• If in doubt, keep out of the way.
• Search the horizon through 360 degrees at least every 5 minutes.

In some ways, commercial fishing boats are an even greater hazard than merchant vessels. At certain times of the year you can encounter large fishing fleets lying to their nets or trolling long lines. Your best strategy is to stay well clear, and to alter course in good time. You can maneuver easily, they cannot. The greatest problem is at night, for fishing boats often display not only the legal lights for the type of fishing in progress, but a welter of spotlights and illuminations that identify them from a long way off and make it difficult to decide which side to pass. Familiarize yourself with major fishing seasons, like the salmon or swordfish months, and plan to avoid the areas where this activity is likely to be concentrated. The coasts off Pacifica, Monterey, Santa Barbara, and much of Southern California are often congested with day fishing boats anchored in or near the kelp. Most fishing boats appreciate you altering course. They have enough to worry about without your help. Incidently, the same boats can give you valuable advice on little known anchorages that provide welcome shelter on windy days, especially north of Point Conception. This book owes a great deal to the insights, friendship, and advice of commercial fishing people. They know the water above and below surface in ways we small boat sailors never do.

MILITARY ACTIVITIES

Whether you like it or not, a large proportion of this nation's defense facilities is concentrated in our cruising area. Two offshore islands, San Nicolas and San Clemente, are off limits to the public. Fortunately, they are relatively far offshore. There are certain restricted and prohibited areas like an army firing range in Monterey Bay. We mention these in the sailing directions chapters. The most obtrusive military areas are the vast segments of the Pacific Missile Range that radiate out to sea from Vandenburg Air Force Base off Points Arguello and Conception and from Point Mugu towards San Nicolas Island. These segments cover the firing tracks of missiles and satellite rockets launched from the mainland. Vandenburg will become the Space Shuttle launching area, a program that may lead to loud sonic booms as well as restricted navigation. Your passage must be timed to cross the Pacific Missile Range at times when it is not in use. If you try to cross during a firing period you will be chased by patrol boats and authoritative aircraft with loud hailers. There is no way you will be allowed to continue until firing is over. You can contact the Duty Range Officers by calling "Plead Control" on Channel 16 (see Chapters 5 and 6). You have, however, a good chance of a clear passage if you time your transits for holidays and weekends when the ranges are generally inactive.

OIL PLATFORMS AND OTHER HAZARDS

Whatever your views on big oil, you must contend with a boom in oil exploration and drilling in our waters. Most oil activity is presently concentrated south of Point Conception. The waters of the Santa Barbara Channel are dotted with enormous oil drilling platforms, surrounded with unlighted mooring buoys. Considerable small boat traffic runs between the rigs and the mainland. For months on end, will be anchored in mid-channel, engaged in exploratory drilling. The positions of fixed platforms are marked on NOS charts, and you should consult *Local Notices to Mariners* for information on new rigs. I have found the platforms to be excellent landmarks in thick weather, especially since they sound 2-second horn blasts every 20 seconds. The oil rigs are well lit with quick flashing lights at each corner and marked with their individual names. If you are tempted to have a close look at an oil rig, stay at least 300 feet away from the platform to avoid trailing lines and gantries. Keep well clear of drilling ships anchored in the channel and off Long Beach. Their anchoring systems can extend up to 5000 feet from the vessel, but are marked by orange and white vertically striped buoys. These are equipped with lights that flash 4 seconds.

Artificial oil islands will be seen off the Rincon near Carpinteria and in Long Beach harbor. These are well lit and should be treated like oil platforms: keep clear. Oil facilities are like commercial shipping, something to be avoided.

A great deal of complex oceanographic research is conducted in California waters. Occasionally you may sight a large drogue or temporary buoys that are not marked on your charts. They may be military markers, or research stations. These short-term marks are identified in *Local Notices,* but few small boat sailors track such advices on a regular basis. Unlit white tanker moorings may be seen close inshore, off oil storage facilities. In a way, all these temporary markers are a hazard, in the sense they can confuse your navigation. The best advice is to rely on permanent navigational marks recorded on up-to-date charts.

An increasing hazard, against which you can do little to protect yourself, is unmarked floating objects. An astonishing amount of flotsam can be seen in California waters: logs from the Pacific Northwest, crates, telegraph poles, oil drums, even semi-submerged containers washed overboard in a distant Pacific storm. Fortunately, most floating debris is relatively innocuous. Large objects like logs are usually readily spotted by day, but represent a formidable hazard at night, when the first warning you may have is the crash as you hit an object at full speed. Your only defense is to keep a sharp lookout, and to be mentally prepared for the possibility of an accidental holing. The remote danger of such a collision is, in my mind, the overriding reason why all passage-making yachts should carry a liferaft. Be encouraged, however: our moderate weather means that far fewer large objects are washed overboard or float away.You are more likely to hit a whale than a submerged object.

STRATEGIES OF PASSAGE-PLANNING: SOUTHBOUND

The success of a longer passage in California depends on careful planning: maximizing prevailing weather conditions to move you north or south, timing your use of tidal streams, and laying off courses that take you clear of hazards, or bring you to the correct spot to make an authoritative landfall. The strategies for completing a southbound passage are quite different from those used to head north. A trip from the Southern California mainland to the offshore islands involves you in another set of variables. Here are some general remarks to help you plan the general outlines of your passage. As with the weather and other phenomena, we describe specific local conditions in later chapters.

Assuming that you time your cruise for a period of settled weather, you will almost certainly enjoy a period of prevailing N to NW winds blowing down the coast. If bound from the Bay area for Southern California on a return voyage, your best strategy is to make the journey in long hops, timing your departure from the Golden Gate for early morning, so that you can make full use of the northerlies as they fill in during the day. With luck, a good breeze will carry you south at a good pace. You are well advised to plan at least one night at sea, making San Simeon, or even better Morro Bay, your first stop.

If the weather is clear, there is a chance that you will carry some wind all night. In foggy months, your chances of a calm night are higher. Whatever the conditions, stay sufficiently offshore to stay well clear of outlying dangers, but well inside the commercial shipping lanes that pass about 10 to 20 miles offshore. The entire coast is lit by well spaced major lights, so navigation should not be a problem.

Bound non-stop for, say, San Diego, you should try to sail past Point Conception in the middle of the day, so that you can make full use of the prevailing tail winds. Be prepared for rough weather, however, and have your reefing gear in order. A good reason to stop at Morro Bay is to be able to choose your weather for Point Conception. On an average day you can clear Morro Bay after breakfast, and be securely anchored in Cojo anchorage in the lee of Conception before sunset. The objective all the way from San Francisco is to make full use of the prevailing winds. Why motor around Point Conception when the wind will take you south for nothing. Unless you are in a hurry, you will be far more comfortable sailing. Why not stop in Morro Bay for a comfortable night and really enjoy the boistrous passage that follows?

Below Point Conception, the winds lighten, as the strong north-westerlies funnel offshore. Even if bound for far Southern California, shape your course through the Santa Barbara Channel rather than outside the islands. You can steer for Santa Cruz Island and Anacapa, which will enable you to ride Windy Lane towards Point Mugu. On no account try to make a landfall on the western end of San Miguel Island, especially in reduced visibility. The area is a morass of unlit rocks, uncharted currents, and submerged dangers. If bound for the islands, spend a night at Cojo and pick your weather for the crossing.

As anyone who races overnight in the south will tell you, the big debate is whether to stay inside near the breakers or to stay offshore when headed towards Los Angeles, San Diego, or Ensenada. Between Port Hueneme and Point Dume, I tend to stay close inshore to make use of any nighttime land breezes. But you can do just as well offshore. During the day, strong westerlies funnel though the channel between Anacapa and the mainland, and your best course lies inshore. Once in the Los Angeles area, plan rhumb line courses to your destination. If bound for San Diego, stay offshore and clear of the commercial shipping bound for San Pedro and Long Beach. Again, keep your stops to a minimum and plan to get south as fast as possible. A pleasant way to reach Ensenada in early May is to stop at Newport Beach and join the annual Newport to Ensenada Race. All you need is a PHRF handicap, provided you enter in advance. The race is not only fun, but a magnificent spectacle. Entrants run the full gamut from ultra-dedicated racing crews to club racers, and dozens of yachts that go along for the spectacle and the partying in Ensenada. It is an unforgettable experience to drift southwards surrounded by hundreds of red and green lights. The Ensenada Race is the ultimate cruise in company, even for the diehard cruising family, especially with gourmet cuisine.

Southbound, you have the advantage of prevailing winds from astern, which enable you to cover the ground fast. You also have the reassurance of dozens of secure ports and anchorages to leeward where you can stop to rest, or run for an emergency. If outward bound on a return journey, never forget that it is going to take much longer to return. Do your harbor-hopping and pottering on the way north to break the monotony of windward passages.

STRATEGIES OF PASSAGE-PLANNING: NORTHBOUND

Only rarely will you be able to sail northwards with a favorable wind. If you do find such a breeze, it will probably be a localized land breeze in the small hours or early morning, or a strong Santa Ana. I have sailed from Santa Barbara Island to Santa Barbara harbor, a distance of 77 miles, in 12½ hours, but this was a unique experience in a cold Santa Ana condition. At times we were reduced to three reefs and the storm jib. A few bold souls use southeasterly gales to make short northerly passages, but this means entering mainland destinations on a lee shore. This can only be described as risky seamanship. Unless you own a light displacement yacht, you should reconcile yourself to long periods of motoring or motor sailing. It is, of course, possible to sail all the way from Ensenada to San Francisco without an engine, but it will take a long time. Even the clumsiest modern yacht will usually make more rapid progress than sailing ships. "We had five days of rainy, stormy weather, under close sail all the time, and were blown several hundred miles off the coast," complained Richard Henry Dana of his first passage from Santa Barbara to Monterey. It took the *Pilgrim* nearly two weeks to make the passage, probably a fairly typical voyage. Under normal conditions, you can expect prolonged periods of calm at night and during the morning hours, with slowly increasing winds during the afternoon until sunset. North of Conception or near the northern offshore islands, you can expect far stronger afternoon winds. Given the prevalence of calm weather, the density of commercial shipping, and the congestion in many marinas and anchorages, I think that serious cruising without an engine is impracticable for anyone with limited vacation time. When northbound, plan on using your engine for long periods. This is when you will bless an autopilot.

Your best strategy northbound is to schedule a port-to-port passage, spacing your anchorages and marinas in such a way that you can cover the mileage under power during the night and morning hours when the winds are quiet. For example, yachts returning from Ensenada to San Diego after the race time their departure for after dinner, motor all night, and arrive in the United States in the early morning. They assume, rightly, that there will be insignificant wind at night. Motoring against a head wind and wind seas is both uncomfortable and a waste of time. Dawdle on the way north. You will end up making much more pleasant progress and the fatigue of perennial headwinds will be reduced.

Some longer northbound passages are inevitable, either because of the spacing of ports and anchorages, or for strategic reasons. For instance, anyone sailing from San Diego to Avalon on Catalina is usually best advised to make an overnight passage from Point Loma to the island under power. You will arrive at Avalon for breakfast. The alternative is to hug the coast and call in at Oceanside and Newport first. This seems a waste of time when you can enjoy these marinas on a downwind cruise home.

Another long northbound passage is through the Santa Barbara Channel. While the southbound yacht is best advised to stay close to the islands, a crew sailing north is probably best off hugging the mainland, visiting Channel Islands harbor and Santa Barbara on the way to Conception and the north. You can reach Santa Barbara from Marina del Rey or King Harbor by motoring outside Anacapa Island during the night and early morning. Just as you reach the Anacapa passage by Santa Cruz, the afternoon westerly will fill in. Then take a long inshore tack under sail alone to Santa Barbara. It is then a 40-mile passage from the city marina to Cojo, an 8-hour journey that is best tackled early in the morning. You can then make use of the offshore gusts that blow seawards from Gaviota Pass.

A successful northbound passage round Conception is a matter of careful timing and choosing settled conditions (Chapter 5). Reconcile yourself to a long motor from Cojo to Morro Bay, most of it at night. From Morro Bay northwards, your best strategy is to hug the coast, following the fathom lines either motoring all the way to Carmel, Monterey, or Santa Cruz in one hop, or using the calm hours and then taking temporary shelter during the windy periods of the day. You will sometimes receive help from a northbound current. Stay inside the 50-fathom line. You will avoid some of the large swells that run further offshore. The best conditions for running north are low cloud days when the seas are oily and the tops of the Big Sur mountains are mantled in fog. Many people leave Morro Bay or San Simeon in the evening, and make an overnight run to Carmel. Beware, however, of small fishing craft close inshore, and of banks of thick fog. This is no coast to take lightly. You should maintain an accurate DR at all times.

Northbound in settled conditions, you are best advised to make for Santa Cruz rather than Monterey, so that you avoid the extra mileage into Monterey Bay. Sailing from Santa Cruz to the Golden Gate can be a bumpy and frustrating experience. Again, your best bet is to stay inshore and make maximal use of temporary anchorages like the bight under Año Nuevo. If you are from Southern California, time your arrival at the Golden Gate for the late morning or early afternoon. You can then lay back and enjoy one of California's great cruising experiences: entering San Francisco Bay under the Golden Gate. Last time we did it, we passed under the bridge in a dense fog with a 20-knot wind behind us. Abruptly the fog lifted like a curtain. We screamed on towards Berkeley in bright, sparkling sunshine. The experience is worth hundreds of miles of motoring to windward.

It is possible to make a non-stop passage from Southern California to San Francisco by tacking over a hundred miles offshore. This route takes you outside the major north-south shipping lanes. Plan your first offshore tack to weather Conception, and take progressively shorter tacks as you make near the Bay area. There is a danger you will run out of wind far offshore, and you may encounter large swells that will inhibit rapid progress. This passage option is only for larger, well-found yachts with experienced crews. Do not attempt this passage in mid-winter. Nor can it be recommended for single-handed sailors.

Most successful northbound passages involve shorter trips and considerable use of one's diesel. You are best advised to plan everything around the northbound legs of your cruise.

MAINLAND TO ISLAND CROSSINGS

Sooner or later, most serious California sailors visit the offshore islands of Southern California. Almost invariably, they reach them after an open-water passage from the mainland of the Santa Barbara Channel or the Los Angeles area. Few yachts cruise non-stop from the north to the islands. The approach is too hazardous in thick weather. North or southbound to the islands, you should follow the strategies for such passages outlined above. But a passage from, say, Newport Beach to Catalina, or from Santa Barbara to Santa Cruz Island, will bring you hard on the wind for the first few hours, then allow you to ease your sails onto a close reach for the last few miles. If you enjoy motoring, plan to leave early in the morning so you are anchored at the islands before the afternoon winds fill in. Those who prefer to sail usually leave about 1100, pick up the strengthening westerlies, and arrive in the late afternoon after 3 to 5 hours sailing. The return passage is normally a comfortable reach. If you depart about noon, the prevailing winds should carry you home in comfortable style.

The major complication of a passage to the islands is the weather condition in Windy Lane, the zone of strong winds that blow down the the islands' inshore side. It may be blowing 30 knots close to

Santa Cruz Island when it is calm at Channel Islands harbor or Ventura. If you are even slightly doubtful about the island winds, try calling a yacht anchored there, or check with the Coast Guard or National Weather Service office. A sure sign of windy conditions offshore: tumbling clouds on the peaks of the islands, or a layer of thick, almost pearly haze at water level on clear days. Be particularly careful on foggy days: the winds can be ferociously strong even when visibility is restricted.

Santa Barbara Island, San Nicolas, and the western offshore islands of Santa Rosa and San Miguel require careful passage- planning. The best way to reach Santa Barbara Island is from Catalina Harbor or Santa Cruz Island, a 40-mile passage over open water. Check the Pacific Missile Range first, and choose settled conditions. Santa Rosa and San Miguel are notorious for strong winds. The best way to reach them is by motoring to windward along the mainland, then crossing from Goleta, Refugio, or Cojo.

In these days of expensive fuel, it makes good economic sense to make full use of the winds that Providence has provided for us to enjoy. With careful planning of your longer passages, you can enjoy California's unique and gorgeous coastline to the full. Throw tightly drawn cruising schedules out of the cockpit, stock up with food and good wine, and enjoy the almost sensuous experience of executing a successful California cruise.

"A bell boat is placed just outside of the bar, in 15 fathoms at mean low water...It is 30 feet long, painted red, and furnished with a day-mark of 3½ feet by 4, elevated 8 feet above the water. The bell weighs 500 pounds, is elevated 15 feet above the water, is rung by the action of the sea... Mariners are cautioned not to run into or damage this aid to navigation..."

—GEORGE DAVIDSON, *Directory* (1858) p.36
(Golden Gate Approaches)

PART II

NORTHERN SAILING DIRECTIONS:
Golden Gate to Cojo Anchorage

"As you go to the northward of the point (Conception), the country becomes more wooded, has a richer appearance, and is better supplied with water."

"We wore round and stood off again, and had the pleasant prospect of beating up to Monterey, a distance of an hundred miles, against a violent head wind. Before night it began to rain; and we had five days of rainy, stormy weather, under close sail all the time, and were blown several hundred miles off the coast."

—*RICHARD HENRY DANA,*
Two Years Before the Mast (1841)

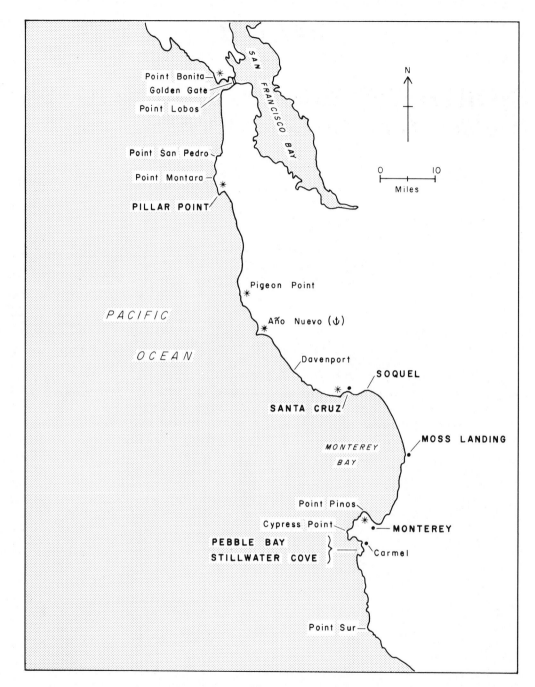

Passage chart: Golden Gate to Point Sur.

Golden Gate to Point Sur

SUMMARY OF PASSAGE STRATEGIES

Passage in and out of the Golden Gate is best timed for periods of favorable stream. You can obtain information on a daily basis from the *Pacific Boating Almanac* or official publications. The best approaches to Golden Gate for small craft are through the Bonita or South Channels, keeping well clear of the busy shipping lanes that run under Golden Gate Bridge.

The coastal passage between Golden Gate and Monterey Bay can be broken at Pillar Point harbor, which requires careful approach on account of the reefs in the entrance. Otherwise, the coastal passage presents no special problems. Northbound yachts should plan the passage for the night or early morning hours, but can take refuge under Año Nuevo when strong headwinds blow.

Año Nuevo is the take-off point for a non-stop passage to Point Sur and points south. A vessel bound for Monterey Bay can make for Santa Cruz harbor as a first stop. However, the entrance to this small harbor can be hazardous in strong SE conditions, and you should check for shoaling in the channel. Monterey Bay itself is often mantled in dense fog, especially early in the morning. Monterey harbor is somewhat out of the way if you are bound to and from the Golden Gate, but is safe in almost any conditions.

Yachts bound from Morro Bay to San Francisco can take shelter in several coves in Carmel Bay, but are better advised to make for Santa Cruz if conditions are quiet, otherwise Monterey. When southbound past Point Sur, you are best advised to leave port early in the morning, so as to arrive off Point Sur about noon. You will then be able to carry the afternoon prevailing winds down the Big Sur coast.

Hazards

Golden Gate is notorious for its strong winds, dense fog banks, and heavy shipping. You should pick your weather very carefully in the winter and spring, when Golden Gate approaches can be very rough indeed. Under normal conditions, your greatest danger is commercial ships. Your best protection is to keep clear of the Traffic Separation Scheme that operates off the Gate, clearly marked on NOS charts.

Dense fog can sometimes be an inconvenience in Monterey Bay, while heavy swells can be encountered off Point Sur.

Passage Times

Assuming an average of 5 knots, you can plan on a passage of about 4 hours from the Golden Gate to Pillar Point harbor, and about 9½ hours from there to Santa Cruz. A non-stop journey from the Gate to Point Sur will consume about thirteen, while the northbound passage will probably take much longer, especially if you encounter strong headwinds. Northbound yachts will take about 7 to 8 hours to motor from Point Sur to Santa Cruz harbor.

Photo: JASON HAILEY

Entering the Golden Gate.

"Its northern shore, composed of high steep rocky cliffs, is the boldest; the southern side is much lower, though its south-eastern point is formed of steep rocky cliffs, from the base of which a tract of sandy country commences..." Thus did the great marine surveyor George Vancouver describe the entrance to the Golden Gate as he entered it in November

1792. The *Discovery* made slow progress against the tide racing out of the entrance and sailed over a shallow bank "as was evident from the confused breaking sea upon it." In Vancouver's day the Golden Gate was much less conspicuous from seaward than it is today. Sir Francis Drake missed the entrance completely. The approach is now dominated by the orange-painted bridge that spans the two shores of the entrance. To sail through the Golden Gate is a magnificent scenic experience, especially on a clear day. As you pass up the narrows, the land closes in on you and the enormous towers of the bridge raise their heads hundreds of feet above your mast. Then, in a few moments, you are through the bridge and the Bay opens up in front of you. If possible sail inland towards the Bay Bridge and enoy the panorama of San Francisco passing to starboard. Even if you are bound for Sausalito or up to the Delta, the deviation is worth it. With its fabulous scenery and coursing tides, the Golden Gate is a fitting northern frontier for our cruising area.

THE GOLDEN GATE (Charts 18680 and 18649)

Entering and leaving the Golden Gate is perfectly straightforward, provided you use the tides and currents to your advantage. The entrance is much used by commercial shipping, and is frequently mantled in constantly moving fog banks. Provided you are prepared for reduced visibility and bumpy seas and keep out of the ship traffic lanes, you should enjoy the Golden Gate.

Approach From Seaward (Chart 18680)

The Golden Gate is readily identified from both north and south in clear weather by a series of useful approach landmarks. These include:
• 23 miles W of the Golden Gate: **the Farallon Islands**, a group of rocky islets that extend NW for 7 miles. Southeast Farallon, the highest land mass, is 350 feet high. Farallon light (Fl. 16 sec. 26 miles) is located here and is an invaluable guide at night. The Farallon radiobeacon (.... F) has a range of 50 miles on 314 kHz. You can anchor in about 50 feet in Fisherman Bay just N of the light, but this is very

much a fair weather berth. Keep well clear of the Fanny Shoal 9.8 miles NW of the light. Noonday Rock, the shallowest part of the shoal, has only 13 feet. A red and black whistle buoy "NR" (Qk. Fl.) lies 0.6 mile W of this danger.

• **Mount Tamalpais**, 7 miles N of Point Bonita, the northern extremity of the entrance, can be seen from as far away as 60 miles. The three summits, the easternmost of which bears a lookout tower, are conspicuous. This densely vegetated mountain contrasts sharply with the surrounding countryside.

• **Point Bonita**, a 100-foot high black cliff, surrounded by high slopes. The white lighthouse (Occ. 4 sec. 18 miles) can be seen from a considerable distance in clear weather. Its radiobeacon broadcasts on 296 kHz (.... B) with a range of ten miles. 100-foot high black and white rock lies a third of a mile to seaward. Point San Pedro is easily recognizable either north or south bound, and is the termination of the Montara mountains inland.

• **Point Lobos**, the southern promontory at the Gate, is a rocky point with a water tank on its summit. The houses of San Francisco and Pacifica stream southwards from Lobos. The Marine Hospital high above the Golden Gate is also conspicuous E of the point.

• The piers of **Golden Gate Bridge** can be discerned above the city as you approach from S, but the bridge as a whole is only visible if you approach from W.

• **San Francisco Approach Lighted Horn Buoy** (SF) lies 9 miles WSW of the entrance. This huge red buoy is 42 feet high and is lit (Fl. 2 sec.). Its radiobeacon broadcasts on 305 kHz (... .... SF) with a range of 17 miles. Buoy SF is the nucleus of the San Francisco Traffic Separation Scheme. Keep well clear of the buoy and the traffic lanes that pass close by.

Your best landmark of all in clear weather is the suburbs of San Francisco that begin at Point San Pedro and end at Point Lobos. Most yachts inbound to the Bay from S will pass fairly close to San Pedro, probably just outside the 10-fathom line. This will bring you to the Golden Gate via the South Channel in about 7 fathoms. The inshore side of this channel is marked by two lit bell buoys, R2 and R4. If you pass close to these markers, you will stay well clear of the southbound traffic lanes offshore. Keep a good lookout for fishing boats and small craft. Unless you have an impelling reason to do otherwise, shape your course inshore. Keep clear of the Traffic Separation Scheme if you possibly can, especially in fog and at night. Another

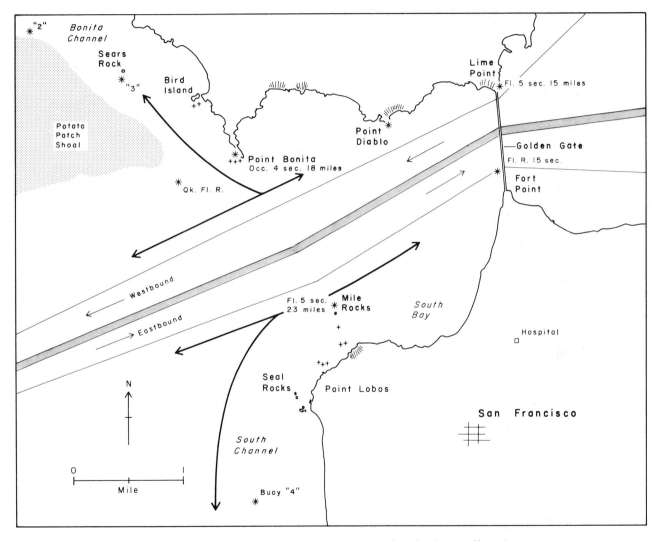

Golden Gate, showing major approach landmarks for small craft.

hazard to avoid is the notorious Potato Patch, a 4-fathom bank immediately NW of the Golden Gate. The best course for southbound small craft is to use the Bonita Channel that passes between the Potato Patch and the shore. Chart 18649 shows the buoys and lights.

San Francisco entrance is hazardous in thick weather. You should rely on radiobeacons:

• Farallon Islands (.... F), 314 kHz, 50 miles.
• Point Bonita (-... B), 296 kHz, 10 miles
• San Francisco Approach Buoy, (... ..... SF), 305 kHz, 17 miles. Bound for the South Channel, your best strategy is to feel your way north along the 10-fathom line until you are off the bluffs south of Lake Merced. If the weather is calm, anchor inshore and wait for clearer weather.

The night approach is straightforward, except for the confusions caused by the multitude of city lights. Identify Farallon light, Point Bonita, and the Approach buoy as you pass N from Point San Pedro. Keep at least a mile off Point Lobos. You will open up Mile Rocks light (Fl. 5 sec.) about 1.5 miles SW of the point. The bridge is marked with Fl. R. 5 sec. on the north side, Fl. R 15 sec. on the south.

Traffic Separation Scheme

The San Francisco Traffic Separation Scheme is designed for the benefit of commercial shipping. It consists of a vessel traffic service of one-way lanes, separation zones, and other devices designed to minimize the risk of collisions and groundings in the Golden Gate. The service is recommended for all vessels over 300 tons. Yachts are exempt from the provisions of the scheme *except* when they enter one of the lanes or zones. The San Francisco scheme is no place for small craft. Make your approach or exit from the Golden Gate *outside* the traffic lanes, which are clearly marked by dotted purple lines on charts 18680 and 16849. *Never* sail in the separation zone between the lanes. If you have to cross the lanes, do so by the shortest possible route. Do not remain becalmed there, and, above all, remember that International

Rules require that you give way to all large vessels in restricted waters. Do not linger near the SF Approach buoy either. It is in this general area that ships alter course for the traffic lanes. The traffic scheme is monitored by the Vessel Traffic Center on channels 13 and 16. You are *not* required to report in to the center.

You may stray close to the southbound traffic lane that passes 3 miles off Point San Pedro. Keep inshore, about 1 mile from land.

Golden Gate Tidal Streams

The Golden Gate is 2 miles wide between Point Bonita and Point Lobos, a narrow, deep-water defile with strong tidal streams that sluice in and out of the entrance. The strongest currents run on either side of the Golden Gate, close to Mile Rocks off Lime and Fort Points, the two termini of the bridge. Violent overfalls may be encountered in these areas, especially when a strong wind is blowing against the tide. Unless you have a very strong engine, you should plan to ride the flood or the ebb through the Gate.

Tidal streams change hourly, and can attain a strength of 6.5 knots under the bridge. The times of maximum ebb and flow can be obtained from daily predictions published in the *Tidal Current Atlas* and *Pacific Boating Almanac*. This admirable publication provides a conversion table as well as hour-by-hour flow charts that enable you to predict the direction and strength of the tides for any hour of the day.

Try to coincide your passage with a favorable tide, or with slack water, which normally occurs for a short period three hours after maximum flood and ebb. Do not attempt passage when a strong wind is blowing against a full contrary tide. Steep seas and overfalls can be very dangerous.

Golden Gate Weather

You are almost certain to encounter some fog and strong winds at the Golden Gate. Spring is the windiest season, with NW breezes of 17 to

30 knots not uncommon as the Pacific High strengthens. Local wind effects can cause gusting, and major shifts. Visibility is usually excellent in spring.

A summer passage will encounter constant N to NW winds that veer and blow out of the W through the Gate. These winds may blow 24 hours a day, between 8 and 10 knots at night, strengthening through the day up to 25 knots or more at the Bay entrance. Night hours can be calm. Fog is commonest in the summer months, to the extent that a permanent fog bank may hover offshore. Fog may appear on the headlands at the Gate in the morning, thicken until early afternoon, and then blow through the bridge with the strengthening wind. The worst fog conditions occur outside the Gate, where foghorns may blow up to 40 percent of the time between July and September. Bound through the Gate in summer, you should try to ride a favorable tide during the afternoon hours.

Foggy conditions are prevalent during summer, and will persist until October. Occasionally, strong NE winds will flow through the Gate, generated by a high pressure system in the Pacific Northwest. This is not weather to sail through the entrance, even if the visibility is perfect.

Winter weather is less predictable because a procession of low pressure systems reach the coast. The strongest winds blow from SE and WNW. They can reach 50 to 75 knots in the approaches. Only 10 to 15 percent of winter days are calm at the Gate. Fog is relatively infrequent, except for occasional radiation fogs that restrict visibility inland and flow out of the Gate. The cooler temperatures and less predictable weather conditions make a winter coastal passage outside the Gate a much less attractive proposition.

Passage Through The Gate (Chart 18649)

The ideal time to transit the entrance is with a favorable tide, or at slack water, on a fog-free summer afternoon However, reality suggests that you will need to compromise. Avoid a passage with a favorable tide against a strong wind. The seas and overfalls have to be seen to be believed. A night passage is entirely practicable, provided you identify Mile Rocks light. Entering or leaving, even when tacking, avoid the traffic lanes in the center of the entrance, and cross them by the shortest route if you must. The tidal streams flow strongest near the shores, but your best course on the south side still lies close outside Mile Rocks light tower. Beware of tidal eddies off Point Lobos and give Seal Rocks a wide berth. There are overfalls of Point Bonita, otherwise the northern shore is straightforward. Keep well clear of the bridge piers. Strong eddies flow around their bases.

Temporary anchorage may be obtained in South Bay off Baker Beach. This is an uncomfortable berth, with tidal eddies and constant wash.

Chart 18649 will enable you to navigate safely within San Francisco Bay. Use the *Pacific Boating Almanac* for details of marinas and facilities.

If you watch your tidal predictions and choose your weather, the passage of the Gate can be an evocative delight.

POINT SAN PEDRO TO AÑO NEUVO (Chart 18680)

The seemingly endless houses of San Francisco and Pacifica extend as far south as Point San Pedro, whose conspicuous off- lying rocks are visible as soon as you clear Point Lobos. The coast is low-lying, with a long sandy beach. On calm days, you may encounter day fishing boats off the beach. Once clear of South Channel, stay near the 10-fathom line. South of Point San Pedro the coast is steep and rocky as far as Point Montara, which exhibits a light (Fl. 5 sec. 16 miles). The point itself is only 60 feet high, but is dangerous because of numerous rocks and reefs that lie up a mile offshore. Keep at least 1.5 miles off the point, passing near to red buoy 10A (Fl.W), which lies that distance offshore. Maintain this distance offshore as you sail past Pillar Point, which lies 18 miles S of the Golden Gate.

Pillar Point is the southern end of a low ridge that extends S from Point Montara. The white radar dish antennas near the summit of the Point can be identified from afar. They offer an excellent landmark north and southbound.

• **Pillar Point Harbor** lies in the N bight of Half Moon Bay, and provides excellent shelter an easy day's sail from San Francisco. The harbor is protected by two long stone breakwaters, lit by two lights, one of which (Fl. 2.5 sec.) is visible for 11 miles.

The approach from N means a wide detour to avoid the ledges and rocks lying off Pillar Point. Pass midway between horn buoy "I" (Fl. G. 2.5 sec.) and Sail Rock outside the 60-fathom line, then shape your

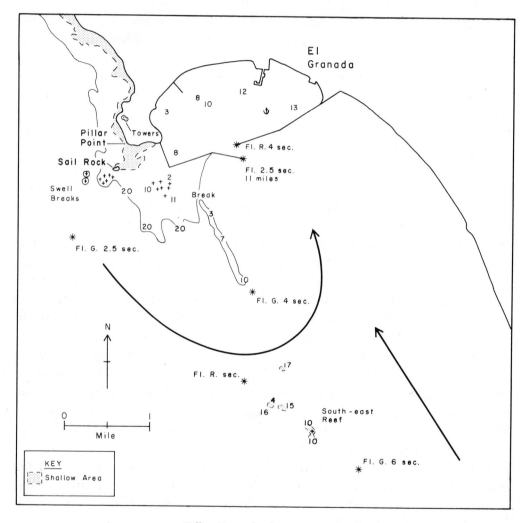

Pillar Point harbor approaches.

course for bell buoy "3" (Fl. G. 4 sec.). For extra safety, plan to turn inshore when the buoy is broad on the port bow. Once inshore of the buoy steer for the entrance, which lies just W of N. Northbound vessels should identify Pillar Point, and then look for the two buoys that mark Southeast Reef. Once these are identified, you can pass either side of the danger area and pass inshore of bell buoy "3". Pillar Point Harbor can be tricky in thick weather or at night, when the buoys are sometimes difficult to identify. The approach is hazardous in strong SE winds.

Visiting yachts must rent a mooring or anchor inside the harbor in 15 to 20 feet sand, beyond them. Do not tie up to a mooring without permission. Water and fuel can be obtained at the L-shaped pier at the head of the harbor.

The coastline between Pillar Point and Santa Cruz harbor consists of high, often yellow bluffs, a short coastal plain, and low, tree covered mountains. The scenery is particularly attractive in the spring and early summer, when the vegetation is green. The coastline trends ESE as you pass the conspicuous smokestack of the Davenport cement works.

• **Pigeon Point** with its powerful light (Fl. 10 sec. 24 miles) and radiobeacon (.... .. (PI), 286 kHz, 40 miles) and Point Año Nuevo are the most useful landmarks on this stretch of coast. Año Nuevo is easily identified by its sand dunes, the detached island just S of the point with its distinctive "skeleton tower" and houses. Pass by at least 1.5 miles off, well outside the lighted buoy (Fl. 6 sec.) that lies S of the tower. Useful temporary anchorage may be obtained immediately S of the light, in a bight protected by the rocks and kelp extending SE from Año Nuevo. Anchor in the smoothest water inshore, with the light bearing about 260 degrees M. You will find 5 to 6 fathoms sand. This anchorage is popular with fishing boats and provides a welcome respite when northbound against strong winds. A strong smell of sea bird droppings emanating from the rocks to windward can infest your berth, however.

• **Año Nuevo** is the moment of decision if you are southbound. A visit to Santa Cruz or Monterey will take you a considerable distance out of your way. If you decide to continue S, lay off a course of 142 degrees M, which will bring you to a position 3 miles W of Point Sur on the far side of Monterey Bay.

The coastal passage to Santa Cruz is extremely pleasant with a commanding breeze. Sail well inside the 20-fathom line and enjoy the interesting rock formations and colorful cliffs, especially at sunset. There are no outlying dangers. If northbound, try to motor this stretch and anchor at Año Nuevo during the windy hours.

MONTEREY BAY (Chart 18865)

Monterey Bay is a diversion from a passage to or from Southern California, but is well worth a few days. The gently sloping shores around Santa Cruz give way to low, sandy topography as the bight curves round 20 miles towards the higher ground behind Monterey. As you approach the bay from the north, you may see an island of hills far to the south, which in fact is the higher land on the far side of the bay. The Salinas Valley and its low, sandy coast do not appear until you are fairly far into Monterey pay. Between July and September, the bay is often fog bound, so that visibility can reach almost zero near Monterey and Santa Cruz at times. Like elsewhere in California, your best advice is to make your passages during the afternoon hours when the visibility may improve to 2 or 3 miles. The prevailing summer winds are W to NW, making much of the bay a lee shore. Bay currents are weak, often rotary, and can be ignored.

• **Santa Cruz Harbor** (Chart 18865) is the northern port in the bay, a delightful place but cursed with a tricky entrance. Your best landmark for the harbor is the town itself, and the city pier, which lies 0.8 miles W of the breakwaters. A night approach is sometimes easier, for you can identify Point Santa Cruz light (Fl. 5 sec. 17 miles) from a long distance away and the breakwaters are inconspicuous against the land. A stranger approaching from the N is best advised to keep outside black and white whistle buoy "SC" which marks rocks and kelp extending SE of the point.

The harbor is protected by two stone breakwaters that protect a channel dredged 20 feet. You can carry about 7½ feet to the road bridge at the head of the harbor. The W breakwater displays an oc-

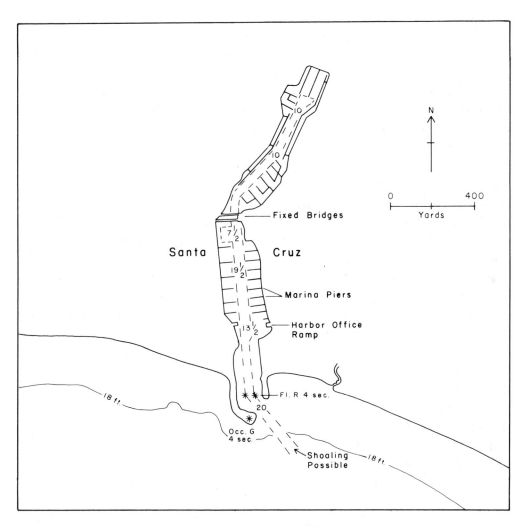

Santa Cruz harbor plan.

culting green light (4 sec), visible at a distance of 6 miles. Santa Cruz entrance is straightforward enough during the summer, but can be dangerous between November and April when SE storms create large ground swells and extensive shoaling at the harbor mouth. *Do not attempt Santa Cruz in rough SE weather or when a high swell is running.* If in doubt, call the Port Director's Office on Channel 12 and

73 during office hours. Night entrance is not recommended for strangers. Anchor off the pier and wait for daylight.

This is a crowded harbor, but visiting yachts can report to the harbor office, at the SE corner of the basin, to obtain a berth. Water, fuel, and repair services are available. Many people prefer to anchor off the pier in 30 feet, sand, a pleasant, relatively smooth anchorage in W conditions, but suicidal in SE weather.

E of Santa Cruz the coastline becomes low-lying and trends to SE, then S. You can anchor in Soquel Cove near Capitola fishing pier and off the point in 15 to 30 feet, sand, near the mouth of Soquel creek. The entrance of the cove is filled with kelp.

• **The Moss Landing** harbor entrance, some 12 miles SSE of Soquel, can be identified by the two 528-foot high smoke-stacks of the power station close inshore. Their red flashing lights are conspicuous at night. Steer for the stacks until you identify the power plant structures, jetties, and offshore pipeline facilities. The entrance is straightforward enough, but you should keep to the N side of the channel to avoid possible shoaling. The harbormaster's office is close to the inner turning basin. They will assign slips if available. There is little to see around Moss Landing, unless you like power plants, or clamming in Elkhorn Slough.

A course of 185 degrees M. will bring you to Monterey harbor entrance (Chart 18685) from Moss Landing.

• **Monterey** is a historic town, dating from the earliest Spanish settlement. The explorer Sebastian Vizcaino wrote to the Council of the Indies about Monterey in December 1602, describing it as an ideal port for repairing deep sea ships. "There is fresh water in quantity and the harbor is very secure against all winds," he wrote. "The land is thickly populated by Indians and is very fertile..." Vancouver visited the Presidio there in 1792, and anchored under the bluff near where the artificial harbor now lies. Richard Henry Dana found Monterey "decidedly the pleasantest and most civilized-looking place in California." The houses were one story adobe structures, the men "always on horseback." It was a "great place for cock-fighting, gambling of all sorts, fandangos, and every kind of amusement and knavery." Dana would not recognize Monterey today. It is a bustling fishing and tourist city, a far cry from Steinbeck's Cannery Row town, although the image is maintained for visitors.

Approaching Monterey from Point Pinos is straightforward in good visibility. Keep at least a mile offshore while rounding the point and along Pacific Grove, or follow the 10-fathom line. The harbor will open up on the starboard bow once bell buoy "4" is just astern. You will use Point Pinos light (Occ. 4 sec. 17 miles) as a long range marker, and buoys "2" and "4" as safe distances off at night. Point Pinos radiobeacon (.... _ PT) broadcasts on 290 kHz to give you a position line.

Monterey Harbor consists of two large breakwaters, the east one forming the municipal wharf. Although small craft can anchor S and SE of the breakwater, the outer harbor tends to be bumpy in strong winds, and, as the Pilot points out: "Loud-barking sea lions usually occupy the breakwater during the day." The Occ. R 4 sec. light at its outer end is easily identified at night.

Yachts normally berth in the inner harbor, the western side of which is formed by a tourist pier with restaurants. Report to the harbormaster's office which is in a trailer at the foot of the municipal wharf. Monterey is usually crowded with fishing boats, and it is often difficult for a visitor to obtain a slip. Fuel and water are available. Excellent repair services.

MONTEREY TO POINT SUR (Chart 18686)

Keep at least 1.5 miles offshore as you pass between rocky Point Pinos and Cypress Point, the northern extremity of Carmel Bay. Cypress is easily identified by its low, wooded appearance and Cypress Point rock, a detached rock 12 feet high lying 450 yards NW of the point.

• **Carmel Bay** can be identified at night by the bright lights of the town. The S side of the bay is bare and rocky, a sandy beach at its head. Carmel Mission lies at the S side of the town and can be identified a long way off.

• You can anchor overnight in **Pebble Bay** or **Stillwater Cove** in about 10 to 20 feet, rock and gravel, but beware of thick kelp and *check your water inlet when anchored and after leaving the anchorage.* Keep a lookout for Pescado Rocks at the entrance to Stillwater. Approaching these bays can be tricky, and is best not attempted without local knowledge. The remainder of Carmel Bay is exposed to prevailing winds. You can shelter in Whalers Cove on the S side of the bay during southerly weather (10 feet gravel and rock), but the approach is foul and the cove full of kelp.

• The 15-mile passage from **Point Lobos** to **Point Sur** is clear of dangers provided you shape your course at least a mile offshore. This can be an exciting sail southbound, as you pick up the strengthening NW wind approaching Point Sur. The steep cliffs of Big Sur gradually give way to less precipitous topography. You can fix your progress by identifying Lobos Rocks off Soberanes Point and the Ventura Rocks 2.2 miles N of Point Sur. By this time the great, isolated black rock of the point will tower ahead, and your passage past Big Sur will lie ahead. Shape your course to pass at least 2 miles off the point, to avoid breakers and rough seas sometimes encountered at this spectacular place.

When northbound, Point Sur is your moment of decision as to whether to head for Monterey or Santa Cruz. Your decision should be based on the strength of the headwinds and the number of hours you have taken to traverse the 50 miles between Piedras Blancas and Point Sur.

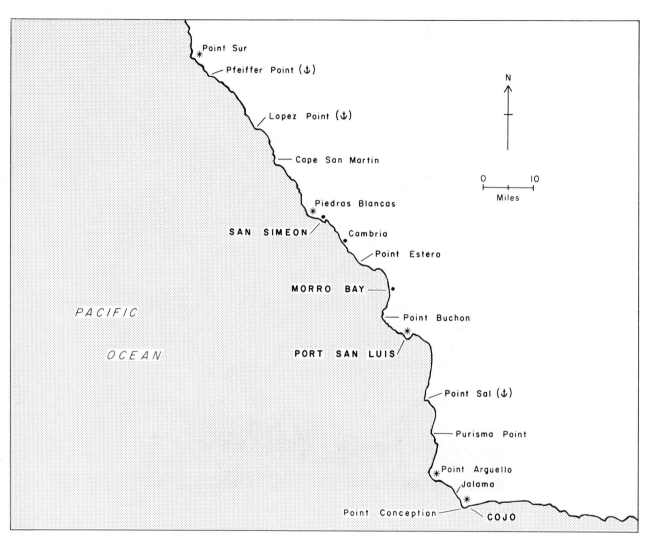

Passage chart: Point Sur to Cojo anchorage.

Point Sur to Cojo Anchorage

SUMMARY OF PASSAGE STRATEGIES

Your best advice is to plan for a non-stop passage along the Big Sur coast between Point Sur and San Simeon or Morro Bay. The few anchorages along this rugged shoreline are, at best, temporary berths. Southbound, you should plan to be off Point Sur about noon, so that you can carry the best of the prevailing afternoon winds for as long as possible. The offshore tack is to be preferred to avoid irritating gybes. Aim to stay about 5 miles offshore. Northbound, you are best advised to stay about 2 miles off the coast, so that you can take refuge in a temporary anchorage if necessary, and make use of any north-flowing current close inshore. Plan on motoring north, if possible in calm conditions. By anchoring in San Simeon Bay, you can schedule your departure for the evening hours and make it an overnight journey, so that you are well past Big Sur in the early morning.

Morro Bay is an excellent harbor except in strong onshore winds, when Port San Luis is to be preferred. The southbound passage past Point Conception is best made in daylight, so that you can use the prevailing tail winds to maximum advantage. Again, use the offshore tack, and gybe inshore once abeam of Conception. Northbound vessels should anchor in Cojo, under the lee of the point to await calm conditions. The winds can blow strongly at Conception any time, but you can often motor N in the night and early morning hours, making for Morro Bay or Port San Luis.

Hazards

Strong winds and poor visibility can hamper a passage past the Big Sur coast Under these conditions, set an offshore course, look out for shipping, and keep plenty of sea room. Under gale conditions, do not take refuge in one of the temporary anchorages, but stay offshore.

Morro Bay entrance is extremely hazardous when high seas are running, and you should go to Port San Luis under these conditions. The latter is exposed to SE gales.

Points Arguello and Conception are notorious for their thick fogs and strong winds. If sailing southbound, you should look out for sudden gusts down the coastal canyons. In rough weather, stay well offshore, where the seas will be more regular, and the gusts less severe. Never attempt to run up this coast before a SE gale. There are no safe refuge harbors within easy reach.

Arguello and Conception lie within the Pacific Missile Range. You should check with the Range Officer before passage.

Passage Times

Assuming an average of 5 knots, a passage from Point Sur to Morro Bay will take about 18 hours. Under normal conditions, you will have wind for about half or more of the passage. Typically, you will be becalmed off Piedras Blancas for part of the night, often in thick fog. The northbound passage time depends on the strength of the head winds.

A southbound journey from Morro Bay to Cojo can be completed in about 12 hours, but the northbound passage may take much longer if there is a swell running.

Point Sur from onshore, from NE, distant 1.0 mile.

"Point Sur, 121 miles NW of Point Arguello and 96 miles SSE of San Francisco Bay entrance, is a black rocky butte 362 feet high with low sand dunes extending E from it for over 0.5 mile. From N or S, it looks like an island and in clear weather is visible for about 25 miles." Thus does the *US Coast Pilot* describe the most conspicuous landmark between San Francisco and Ensenada. The illusion of an island is strong and makes Point Sur easy to identify from a distance. This is an important landmark for both north and southbound yachts. The southbound vessel is now committed to a long passage to either San Simeon Bay or Morro Bay, unless bound even further south.

THE BIG SUR PASSAGE.

The southbound passage is best timed to give you the best of the day's prevailing winds down the coast from Point Sur. A typical passage will involve a fairly boisterous ride, with the wind dead astern. The magnificent scenery, of jagged mountains and steep cliffs, forested hills and dramatic road cuts, more than compensates for the discomfort. This is an ironbound coast. Your best advice southbound is to lay a course that takes you on the offshore gybe. When the wind abates or you have sufficient southing, you can then steer inshore for your destination. A more inshore course passing, say, within 1.5 miles of Piedras Blancas, may involve you in frequent rough water gybes, and a lot of unnecessary discomfort. If you are bound all the way to Conception, steer the rhumb line course, and maintain distant visual contact with the land.

In all likelihood you will experience reduced visibility on this leg of your passage. George Vancouver enjoyed typical conditions in 1792: "The fog did not in general rise more than ten or twelve degrees above the horizon; above which the atmosphere was clear and pleasant, admitting us frequently to see not only the summits, but also some distance down the sides of the mountains that compose on the coast." If you are lucky enough to enjoy clear weather, make some sketches of the profiles of the mountain tops: they are a useful check on your DR when offshore.

If you aim to round Point Sur in the late morning, you should carry the wind, *under average conditions,* well down the coast. Your offshore course will keep you clear of dangers during the calm and foggy night hours. Once you have run your DR distance, you can alter course inshore and arrive near your destination as the fog lifts the next day.

When bound up the Big Sur coast *stay inshore*, passing within 1.5 miles of Piedras Blancas and Point Sur. Time as much of the passage as possible for the night and early morning, and only attempt it in calm weather. Typically, this will be foggy weather, or low overcast, when the base of the cliffs are visible. An inshore passage lets you keep precise track of your position and run into the very occasional temporary shelter anchorages along this inhospitable coast. You may also receive some help from the northbound inshore current. Do not attempt a close inshore passage unless you have a reliable engine. If a strong headwind develops and you are not close to an anchorage, set a long tack offshore and sail clear of the lee shore.

A useful series of major landmarks will help you maintain an accurate DR even in foggy conditions. These are, from N to S:

• **Point Sur** (Fl. 15 sec. 22 miles) has a radiobeacon (.__. ... PS) on 320 kHz with a range of 50 miles.

• **Pfeiffer Point** lies 6 miles SE of Point Sur, the seaward termination of a 2,000 foot high ridge. Pfeiffer's bold, light-colored face stands out clearly from some distance to the S. This is an important landmark because of the shelter anchorage under its lee.

• Two hills, **Twin Peak and Cone Peak,** lie 4 miles NE of Lopez Point. The scattered trees on their summits are easily identified. There is an observation tower on Cone Peak.

• **Cape San Martin,** 27 miles SE of Pfeiffer and 16 miles NW of Piedras Blancas, is lit (Fl. 6 sec. 7 miles) from a small, inconspicuous tower 200 feet above the ocean. This is a faint light, one that I have only spotted once during several inshore night passages. The San Martin Rocks lie close offshore and provide an easy way of spotting this point from S. The innermost rock is 144 feet high. Its white color is conspicuous. The Willow Creek bridge of Highway 1, 0.3 miles N, is a good landmark when abeam of the point.

• **White Rocks,** two conspicuous isolated rocks 3.8 and 4.5 miles SE of San Martin.

• **Point Piedras Blancas** (chart 18700; *ChartGuide* p. C1) marks the S end of the Big Sur coast. The low, rocky headland projects 0.5 mile from the coast. Two large and conspicuous white rocks lie 500 yards offshore, giving the point its name. Keep well off Piedras Blancas, preferably outside the lighted horn buoy "4A" (Fl. R 4 sec.). Piedras Blancas light (Fl. 10 sec. 25 miles) is a major landmark. The lighthouse compound is conspicuous. The radiobeacon (.__. .__. PB) has a range of 10 miles on 296 kHz.

You have the option of a number of temporary anchorages along the Big Sur coast, as follows:

• **Pfeiffer Point** offers protection in N to NW conditions about 0.9 mile ESE of the point. Anchor in about 30 to 50 feet in sand, SW of Wreck Beach, which is marked on chart 18686. This anchorage is much used by fishing boats, and can be recommended in quite windy conditions. Beware of kelp and lay plenty of scope. Use this anchorage in preference to Point Sur.

Photo: PETER HOWORTH

Big Sur coast: Point Lopez from S.

Photo: JASON HAILEY

Piedras Blancas light, bearing NE, distant 0.6 mile.

• **Lopez Point.** Anchor a mile SE of the point either just inside or just outside the kelp bed in 30 feet or more. The light should bear about 275 degrees M. Beware of a submerged rock 0.5 mile SE of the point. Heavy swells can roll in here. A temporary anchorage used by fishing boats.

• **Piedras Blancas.** Anchorage may be obtained under the lee of the point in and NW conditions, in 20 to 30 feet, sand and rock. This is a tricky anchorage to approach without local knowledge. Use in calm weather only. San Simeon Bay, only 5 miles away, is vastly preferable. You can also anchor SE of La Cruz Rock, 3 miles NNW of Piedras Blancas, a berth said to be safe in strong NW winds.

It is best to count on a long passage past the Sur coast. Pfeiffer is the only reliable anchorage in anything of a blow.

SAN SIMEON BAY (Chart 18700; *ChartGuide, p.C1*)

Hearst Castle, a remarkable palace by any standards, will be spotted high above Piedras Blancas on a clear day. Any leisured cruise should include a visit to this extraordinary edifice. You can walk up to the entrance from San Simeon Bay, 5 miles SE of Piedras Blancas.

The mountains recede from the coastline at Piedras Blancas, which becomes a rolling coastal plain with low cliffs and off-lying rocks and sandy beaches all the way to Morro Bay, 27 miles SE. Keep at least a mile offshore the entire way. Well- wooded San Simeon Point is easily identified from N. Approach the anchorage by rounding the lighted bell buoy (Fl. 6 sec.) 0.4 mile SE of the point. Northbound, you will probably spot the buildings of the small settlement and the pier first.

San Simeon Bay provides good protection in prevailing N and NW conditions, except when a heavy swell rolls around the point. It is completely exposed to SE gales. Anchor in the middle of the bay in 20 to 35 feet, hard sand. Lay plenty of scope and make sure your anchor is well dug in. You will probably share the bay with a couple of fishing boats. Land at the pier, an operation that takes care when the swell is running, or dinghy to the SW corner of the beach in calm conditions. This is an excellent anchorage for waiting for good conditions to transit the Big Sur coast. Do not, however, attempt a night approach without local knowledge.

San Simeon Bay from SW, distant about 1.0 mile. Clear entrance to the anchorage can be obtained by steering for the white buildings back of the beach. Two yachts can be seen anchored in the best spot.

Photo: JASON HAILEY

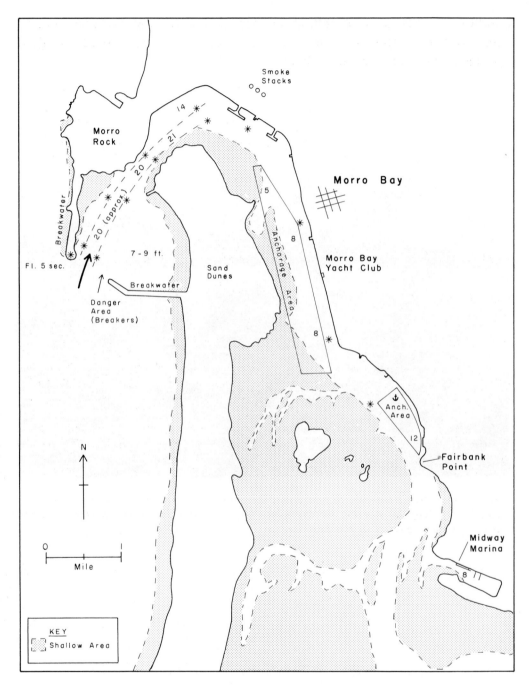

Morro Bay harbor plan.

MORRO BAY (Chart 18703; *ChartGuide*, pp.C3-6)

The coastline between San Simeon and Morro Bay has little to offer the small yacht. You should stay near the 30-fathom line past Cambria and Point Estero. The passage to Morro Bay is a nice day sail, and particularly attractive at sunset. Two white radar domes are a good landmark 5 miles NW of Estero. So is White Rock 6 miles NW of the same point. Keep a sharp lookout for Von Helm Rock off Cambria, which is marked by a red gong buoy "4" (Fl. 6 sec.). Pass outside this danger.

As you near Estero, you should identify Morro Rock, another famous landmark on this coast. Shape your course to pass 1.5 miles to seaward, and avoid the rocks and oil facilities in Estero Bay. A northbound vessel will have no problem identifying the harbor entrance from the same landmark. Another useful landmark: three 450-foot high power plant stacks which display flashing red lights at night. Provided you keep 1.5 miles offshore, the approach to Morro Bay presents no problems in normal weather. However, everyone should approach the entrance itself from SW, to minimize effects of currents and swells, especially in strong winds. It is not, however, a harbor to enter in rough weather when the swells in the entrance reach formidable proportions. Under these conditions, divert to Port San Luis, or stay offshore.

Morro Bay is a delightful harbor, one of my favorites on the entire California coast. With its busy fishing traffic, pleasant, working waterfront, and low key atmosphere, Morro Bay is reminiscent of many European fishing villages. Plan to spend several days in this delightful place.

The harbor entrance lies between two protective breakwaters. The channel between them is buoyed, and carries a depth between 16 and 10 feet right into the port. The swell can break across the entire entrance at low tide under some conditions, so plan your arrival for near high water. The harbormaster monitors Channel 16 and can brief you on entrance conditions. Note that the area around Point Estero is one of the foggiest on the coast. If in doubt about the position of the entrance, sound your way to the 10- fathom line and anchor until the weather clears. Do not hang around the entrance in thick weather: fishing boats leave at full speed.

Photo: JASON HAILEY

Morro Bay entrance, distant 0.5 mile, showing three smokestacks, Morro Rock, breakwater, and channel buoys. The best water is on the northern side of the channel.

The entrance channel leads under the shadow of Morro Rock and trends past a low, sandy point to the S. The tide runs between 2 and 4 knots in the channel, especially on the ebb. Stay within the channel, and keep towards the port side as you pass up the channel, especially at low tide. The deepest water normally lies towards the town and under the rock. The boats on moorings are normally close to aground at low water. Berthing space for visitors is rather limited, but you should consult the harbormaster. It is sometimes possible to tie up at the city dock, or, by prior arrangement, with Morro Bay Yacht Club. The White Point Marina is operated by Morro Bay State Park, and carries about 4 feet at low water. There are also some private marinas (see *Pacific Boating Almanac)*. You can anchor off, but may have some difficulty finding deep water out of the channel and the strong stream.

Morro Bay is accessible at night. You should identify the light on the N breakwater (Fl. 5 sec. 17 miles), then follow the lighted channel. The radiobeacon (-- M) is audible on 310 kHz for 15 miles. Note that the signal is unreliable E of a line bearing 291 degrees M from the light.

A final word of caution. Avoid Morro Bay in rough weather. The entrance can be extremely dangerous.

PORT SAN LUIS (Chart 18703; *ChartGuide,* pp.D1-2)

The coastline between Morro Bay and Port San Luis is steep-to and hilly. The dominant landmark is Saddle Peak, 4.1 miles NNW of Point San Luis, which can be seen from over 40 miles away on a clear day. You can pass within 1.5 miles of the coastline between Point Buchon and Port San Luis. If making a landfall on this stretch of coast in reduced visibility, the Diablo Canyon nuclear power plant's white domes are a useful signpost, as is Lion Rock, a detached 136-foot high rock 2.6 miles SE of Point Buchon.

Port San Luis, just SW of the town of Avila, is a little out of the way for a yacht bound up and down the coast. In heavy weather, it is preferable to Morro Bay with its hazardous entrance. The port is little more than an open roadstead protected by a breakwater on the SW side. The approach from S is straightforward. Identify Saddle Peak, and Point San Luis, the prominent headland with the protective breakwater at its foot. Point San Luis light (Fl. 5 sec) is visible 24 miles away, a useful guide when northbound at night from Point Conception. The radiobeacon (... .... SL) broadcasts on 288 kHz with a range of 20 miles. Southbound vessels should shape a course to stay clear of Santa Rosa Reef and the kelp beds that extend SW from

Lone Black Rock. Entering the harbor, keep well to starboard of Lansing Rock, which is buoyed. Anchorage may be obtained over a muddy bottom in 18 to 30 feet, S of Port San Luis wharf. Keep clear of mooring chains and lay plenty of scope. Apply to the harbormaster's office by the wharf for a guest mooring. Fuel, water, and repairs available.

Port San Luis offers good shelter in N to NW conditions, but is very rough in SE storms.

POINTS ARGUELLO AND CONCEPTION
(Chart 18721; *ChartGuide* pp.D3-4)

The stretch of California coast between Points Arguello and Conception has earned an evil reputation from cruising sailors for its strong winds and rolling swells. Conception is often called, somewhat grandiloquently, the "Cape Horn of the Pacific." George Davidson called it "a peculiar and remarkable headland...Once seen it will never be forgotten...We have frequently seen vessels coming from the eastward with all sail set, and light airs from the north, in very little time reduced to short canvas upon approaching the cape, and vessels from the northwest coming before a spanking breeze lose it within a few miles after passing the cape." The 60 miles between Morro Bay and Conception loom as a major obstacle in the minds of everyone cruising along the coast. Certainly, Conception is no place for the novice. But there is no reason why a well-found yacht should not round the point in perfect safety.

Arguello and Conception lie in a magnificent natural setting. S of Port San Luis, the coast is low-lying beach and sand dunes, culminating in Point Sal, a bold, dark headland, which looks like a low conical hill from NW. Anchorage may be obtained under Point Sal in 35 to 40 feet, sand. This place was a popular anchorage for loading hides and tallow in the nineteenth century. From Point Sal, the coast continues low and sandy, turning low and rocky near Purisima Point, 10.6 miles N of Arguello. Keep well clear of this stretch of coast. Onshore currents frequent this vicinity, and swells close inshore can be extremely dangerous. The seaward end of the Santa Ynez mountains is near Arguello. The 2170-foot Tranquillon mountain can be seen behind the jagged, rocky promontory. Arguello is inconspicuous and rocky, projecting about 800 yards W of the coast as a whole. The small light structure exhibits a powerful flash (Gp. Fl. 2 30 sec.) visible from 26 miles away. The radiobeacon (.__ O) broadcasts on 302 kHz. The point is unmistakable because of the huge missile gantries that rise like silent monoliths close inland. The railroad passes immediately inshore of the coastline. I once sailed close inshore at Arguello on a quiet summer's evening. The visibility was perfect, the wind a soft 10 knots. Even the swells were minimal, birds fishing from the weathered rocks close to the water's edge. The landscape resembled a moonscape of razor-sharp rocks, desolate grass, and the ever present sounds of the Pacific. The missile gantries towered high above us, silent and menacing in the soft light. Arguello was a surrealistic experience, and an awesome place even on a calm evening. This is no place to be caught on a lee shore. No sane sailor should approach this headland under anything but calm conditions.

The coastline now forms a large bight of low cliffs and sandy beaches. Arlight refuge harbor lies 3.5 miles SE of Arguello, little more than a shallow bay behind a rock breakwater. Do not use this refuge except in grave emergency, and *avoid the area at all costs even in moderately windy weather.* The shallow water swells on this coast must be seen to believed. Anchorage may be obtained inside the kelp off Jalama State Beach, but only in quiet conditions. Conception lies 12 miles S, a bold headland with relatively low land behind it, so much so that you can confuse it for an island from offshore. The light (Fl. 30 sec. 26 miles) is displayed from a 52-foot high tower behind a house at the W end of the point. The land trends to the at the point as you enter the Santa Barbara Channel. Beware of a low, black rock 220 yards SW of the light, "upon which some of the California steamers have struck in very foggy weather," wrote Davidson.

Photo: GRAHAM POMEROY

Point Conception from NW, distant 0.5 mile.

Conception Weather

Point Conception, like Cape Flattery, Washington, or Cabo San Lucas in Baja, is a bold edge to a major landmass, a promontory backed by mountains that act as a barrier against the prevailing winds. Its cliffs are an abrupt interruption of the steady onshore winds and of Pacific swells that have been thousands of miles in the making. Thus, local weather conditions can differ drastically from those a few miles away. It is these unusual circumstances that make the waters around the point so notorious.

Daylight calms are unusual between Arguello and Conception. When offshore winds are relatively stable and cool, the point causes the air to lift some seven to nine times the height of the Cape to windward, leaving a fluky area immediately windward of the promontory. Both wind and sea conditions quiet down, and you can enjoy an idyllic

Photo: GRAHAM POMEROY

Point Conception from E, distant 1.0 mile.

passage around the Cape. Once I sailed close offshore on a calm evening when the wind was barely 10 knots and the entire landscape was bathed in pink, sunset light. I felt uneasy, for it was as if Conception was holding its breath, gaining strength for another day.

If offshore conditions are unstable, and frontal systems or pressure changes threaten far out in the Pacific, there is no lifting and the onshore winds hit the Cape in full force. The air compresses, then squeezes past the point in a funnel effect that channels it through a small area at the land. This causes wind velocity to increase sharply. As a general rule, coastal winds tend to lie down late at night or in the small hours, then pick up during the morning and strengthen during afternoon and evening. The diurnal cycle starts with offshore winds that blow at dawn and dusk when the land cools down (see Chapter 2 for veil clouds and related phenomena). Then the onshore winds fill in and increase as the sun begins to heat the land. Warm air rises in a thermal effect, a sea breeze circulation now causes lower pressure at Point Conception, and the onshore wind accelerates to fill the gap. Offshore, the downflow of the sea breeze brings gustier, upper level air down to the surface. Under these unstable conditions, Point Conception winds can be 50 to 130 percent higher than offshore winds. In other words, an 18 knot wind offshore can have a local velocity at Conception as high as 42 knots. Strong gusts, irregular swells, and wind waves accentuate heavy weather conditions off the point. Great swells refract off the cliffs and can hit you in several directions at once.

My first southbound passage around Conception was in a 32-foot, heavy displacement sloop. Four miles NW of the point we broached-to under a reefed main and small jib when a gust hit us at the same time as a confused swell on the quarter. The cockpit flooded. It took an hour to clear up the mess below. Had we not been wearing safety harnesses, someone would have gone overboard. So exaggerated are local conditions that a giant wind shadow can extend up to 20 or 30 times the height of the point away from the land to windward. You can be taken aback in a few seconds as you sail into the shadow.

Fog is a major problem past Conception. You can count on between 12 and 20 foggy days a month at Arguello between June and October, days with visibility of less than 0.5 mile. The worst months are September and October. Foggy conditions are highly localized, so that Conception can be clear while Arguello is fog-bound. Although wind conditions tend to be quieter on foggy days, this is not an invariable rule.

• The southbound passage is best made from Morro Bay, for Port San Luis is out of your way. Aim to leave harbor after a leisurely breakfast, and shape your course to pass at least 2 miles off Point Conception. Under normal conditions, prevailing winds will be astern and will fill in during the day. Assume you will experience heavy weather, and be prepared to reef in a hurry. Remember that offshore winds can blow down the canyons at dawn and dusk. As you bring Arguello broad on the port bow, tuck in your first reef as a precaution, and ride the afternoon wind past Conception. Be prepared for strong gusts, rough seas, and set an offshore course if you are on a gybing run. Do not make the mistake of being sucked in near the coast on the inshore tack. A well-found yacht will have no trouble with a daylight transit of the area, and should experience winds that will not exceed 30 knots. If the wind is blowing in this range early in the morning at Morro Bay, or you think conditions are too rough for a day passage, you will often find quieter conditions, perhaps in the 20 knot range, at night.

If you prefer quiet conditions, plan the passage for night or very early morning hours. Arguello and Conception are well lit. Watch for sudden fog banks, gusty offshore winds, and veil clouds. Maintain an accurate DR position. Use the 50 fathom line when bound past these headlands in thick weather.

• Northbound, pick your weather carefully. Aim to round the point in the small hours and reconcile yourself to motoring the whole way. A good strategy is to leave Santa Barbara in early morning, and arrive at Cojo anchorage just E of Conception in the late afternoon. Once at Cojo, enjoy a leisurely dinner and a short sleep. Then up anchor at midnight and round Conception about 1.5 miles offshore. If conditions are calm, you will experience some bumpy swells, but be closing Morro Bay by mid-morning. Be prepared, however, for a wait. You might be forced to remain in Cojo for several days before conditions are suitable, even at midnight. Both fog and wind should shape your decision. Do not hesitate to return if you find open water conditions unsuitable.

When bound non-stop from Northern California past Conception, your best course lies about 5 to 7 miles offshore, where you will miss the worst of the confused seas off the point. Keep a sharp lookout for ships in this vicinity.

Before departing on a passage past Conception, check the Vandenburg firing schedule on Channel 16 "Frontier Control," or by calling (805) 865-3405 or 3406, Mondays to Fridays, 0800 to 1600.

Cojo Anchorage

Cojo anchorage has been an important refuge for centuries. The Spaniards preferred it to Santa Barbara, nineteenth-century whaling ships processed their catches on the beach. "There is a large rancho," wrote George Davidson in 1858. "It is one of the very best tracts for grazing. The beef has a finer flavor and more delicacy than any we have met with on the coast." There was good firewood, but "disagreeable" drinking water.

Cojo lies immediately E of Government Point, a lowlying, rocky promontory a mile E of Conception. You can identify the anchorage from a low, brown cliff on its W side, and a conspicuous railroad culvert at the head of the beach at the foot of an embankment. Anchor under the lee of the cliff opposite the culvert in 20 to 35 feet, sand. Look out for the dense kelp that often lies in the entrance, and lay plenty of scope. Sudden swells can roll in during the night. You should allow plenty of swinging room to stay clear of other vessels. Do not be tempted to anchor too close to Government Point, where there is a wreck in 30 feet and swells tuck around the corner, or in Little Cojo, identified by an oil storage tank. The bottom is foul.

Cojo is an ideal place to wait for a passage around Conception and to plan a satisfying cruise among California's offshore islands.

PART III

SOUTHERN SAILING DIRECTIONS:
Santa Barbara Channel to Ensenada

"Off this part of the coast to the westward (of Santa Barbara) we experienced a very extraordinary sensation, as if the ship was on fire, and after a very close investigation attributed it to a scent from the shore...it occurred to me that it might arise from naphtha on the surface."
—SIR EDWARD BELCHER, 1839

"Navigators, in making the Santa Barbara channel from the northwest, readily estimate their approach in thick foggy weather by the peculiar odor of the bitumen which, issuing from a large pit on the shore about 8 miles west of Santa Barbara and floating on the water, works against the summer winds far beyond Point Conception."
—GEORGE DAVIDSON, 1858

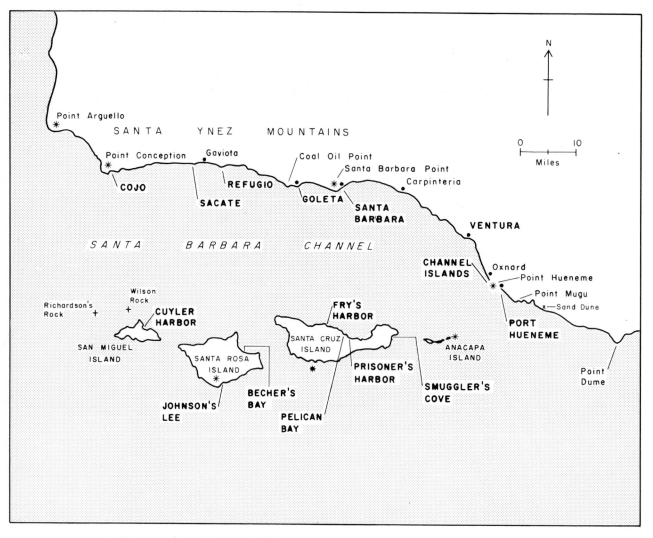

*Passage chart: Cojo anchorage to Point Dume, including offshore islands.
Islands omitted for clarity.*

Santa Barbara Channel to Point Dume Including Offshore Islands

CHAPTER 6

SUMMARY OF PASSAGE STRATEGIES

Southbound passages from Point Conception non-stop to Los Angeles or beyond are best shaped to pass well offshore of Conception and clear of out-lying dangers on N coasts of San Miguel and Santa Rosa Islands. Aim to pass inside Windy Lane, which extends about 6 miles inshore of the islands to maximize prevailing following winds. Refuge anchorages will be found on the N shore of Santa Cruz. Prevailing winds funnel between Anacapa Island and the mainland. Plan to follow rhumb line from Santa Barbara Channel to Los Angeles area. If bound for San Diego, pass close to N coast of Catalina Island. Check the Pacific Missile Range on Channel 16 before traversing firing areas.

Northbound, aim to break the journey and to power to windward during calm night and early morning hours. A good course from Los Angeles will take you outside Anacapa during the night, then through Anacapa Passage in late morning to pick up the afternoon westerly across to Santa Barbara. You can then motor to Conception close inshore.

The same northbound strategy applies when planning an island cruise. Make your windward mileage by hugging the mainland, then cross to San Miguel Island or Santa Cruz from Cojo, Sacate, or some other windward anchorage. You then have a wide choice of anchorages on both coasts of the islands, and a minimum of windward passage-making.

Steady NW winds will be found 20 miles S of the Channel Islands under normal conditions, but such a course is only recommended for really long distance passages.

Hazards

Heavy shipping traffic can be encountered in the Santa Barbara Channel, passing through a Traffic Separation Zone just outside Windy Lane. Keep outside this zone, and cross it at the correct angle if bound to and from the mainland. Oil platforms and drilling ships dot Channel waters and should be avoided. The Santa Barbara Channel can be hazardous in strong NE conditions. You should be prepared to clear out of island anchorages at short notice if dry, calm conditions and slight ground swell herald a possible NE blow.

Passage Times

Assuming an average of 5 knots, you can sail from Cojo anchorage or San Miguel Island to Santa Barbara in about 8 hours, and from Santa Barbara to Pelican Bay on Santa Cruz island in about 5. The transit of the entire Santa Barbara Channel will take about 12 hours under normal westerly conditions, and will include some motoring. A passage from Channel Islands to Santa Barbara harbor takes about 5 hours under power, and slightly less sailing to leeward from Santa Barbara. Most destinations within the Channel are within an easy day's sail.

Santa Barbara Channel and its approaches are probably the most attractive cruising ground in California. The channel offers picturesque towns, sheltered waters, and a feast of remote and unspoiled anchorages to satisfy the most demanding of cruising gourmets. I have described the ports and anchorages of this fascinating area with Graham Pomeroy in the *Cruising Guide to the Channel Islands* (Capra Press, Santa Barbara, and Western Marine, Ventura, 1979). This volume contains detailed sailing directions for both the mainland and the offshore islands and it is pointless to repeat the detailed descriptions in that book here. Since this is a passage-making guide, I will confine myself to general remarks about the strategies of cruising and passage-making between Cojo anchorage and the Los Angeles area.

GENERAL PASSAGE-MAKING STRATEGIES FOR THE AREA
(Chart 18720; *Chart Kit* pp.2-3; *ChartGuide*, pp.F1-2)

The strategies of passage-making in the Santa Barbara Channel and among the offshore islands are determined by the prevailing winds, which blow from W to E. The vast majority of yachts cruising this area approach it from SE, and face a long windward passage to the islands. Under normal conditions the sailing conditions in the channel are relatively predictable. You can count on calm weather for the night and early morning hours, and on steady westerlies that fill in during the late morning. The strongest winds blow in SE storms during Santa Anas from NE, and after frontal passage from W and NW. Offshore, down canyon winds can present a hazard, especially in fall and winter months. The strategies of passage-making in this area are simple:

• Make windward progress during night and morning hours when winds are calm.

• Use the prevailing winds to carry you from anchorage to anchorage downwind.

• On a circular cruise, hug the mainland when bound upwind, the islands when sailing towards Los Angeles.

• Anchor with extreme care in dry NE weather conditions, when the channel and its anchorages can be suicidal.

• Keep away from the mainland in SE gales; nearly all ports are dangerous lee shores.

SOUTHBOUND PASSAGE-MAKING

Unless bound for southern latitudes far offshore, the southbound yacht sailing non-stop for Los Angeles or further S is certain to pass through the Santa Barbara Channel. A passage outside San Miguel and the other offshore islands that protect the channel is not recommended, for the prevailing winds tend to be lighter, and except well S of the islands, you normally save no time. The non-stop course is best shaped to pass within 5 miles of the N shores of San Miguel, Santa Rosa, and Santa Cruz Islands. You can then ride downwind in Windy Lane, the zone of stronger winds that funnels down the channel from Point Conception. This course has the advantage of a number of secure refuge anchorages to starboard, anchorages that are secure in SE gales and post-frontal winds. You may also pick up a few miles from the E-bound rotary current that is sometimes claimed to flow in the outer waters of the channel. Lay off a course that passes between the traffic separation zones through the channel and the islands. You may encounter rough seas and strong winds, but should enjoy a fast passage past some magnificent scenery. And you can easily divert into, say, Bechers Bay on Santa Rosa or Pelican Bay in Santa Cruz, if becalmed. You can catch up on some precious sleep while waiting for the stern winds to blow in late in the day. A non-stop course will take you inside Anacapa Island and a few miles offshore to the Los Angeles area. This can be a fine passage if you time it for the afternoon winds.

   Your major landmarks for such a passage are:

• San Miguel Island, to starboard. Its white, sandy cliffs are distinctive, as are the twin humps of its low hill.

• Lowlying Santa Rosa Island, close E of San Miguel. This island has a long, tapering W end.

• W end of Santa Cruz Island, which looks like a peak from a considerable distance. The N coast will open up as you approach.

• To port, a backdrop of the Santa Ynez mountains. You can discern their summits even on hazy days. Few other details of the mainland will be visible.

• Anacapa Island will emerge into view from behind Santa Cruz when you are well down the N coast of the latter. The W end of the island rises to a peak, and is highly characteristic.

• The mountain range behind Oxnard, E of Point Mugu. These peaks will appear up to 40 miles away on a clear day. The sandy plains by Point Hueneme will not appear until you are within 10 miles of the coast.

If you are southbound with more leisurely plans, spend at least one night at Cojo anchorage. As a precaution, make sure you have provisioned your boat at a northern port for a cruise of several days, perhaps a week or more. You have several options to choose from:

• A passage to Santa Barbara and then across to the islands. This will mean a downwind run to Santa Barbara, then a close fetch to Santa Cruz Island. A visit to San Miguel and Santa Rosa will then involve some tiresome windward work.

• To cross from Cojo or Sacate to San Miguel Island, then working your way E down the islands, crossing from Santa Cruz to Santa Barbara, or taking in the mainland upon your return journey.

• A direct passage to Santa Cruz Island from Cojo in Windy Lane, missing the W islands.

Anyone planning a serious island cruise should choose the second option. Cojo is to windward of all the islands. You can reach across to Cuyler Harbor on San Miguel, a mere 22 miles, in 3 to 4 hours. This will be a windy passage, but winds will be abeam and a well reefed-down yacht should set out in the early morning to reach Cuyler before the breeze reaches full strength. The only hazard on this passage is Wilson Rock, 2.2 miles NW of Harris Point, your landmark for locating Cuyler Harbor. Do not make this passage at night. San Miguel is unlit. Having enjoyed San Miguel Island, you can then sail slowly to leeward, taking in the south coast of Santa Rosa island, and then exploring Santa Cruz Island from a windward vantage. When your island cruise is over, you can sail across to Channel Islands harbor, Ventura, or Santa Barbara and make your way back to windward along the mainland coast.

To sail direct to Santa Cruz is simply a matter of your personal preference and available time. You can sail from Cojo to Fry's Harbor or Bechers in a comfortable day, provided you leave relatively early in the day. This option will give you more time in Santa Cruz' beautiful coves.

Unless you have an impelling reason to visit Santa Barbara, plan on first exploring the island anchorages that lie upwind of the harbor. Time and again, I meet visitors who have sailed from Cojo to Santa Barbara and then decide to visit San Miguel or the W end of Santa Cruz island. Now they are now faced with a dreary windward passage which they could have avoided by sailing across to the islands from the upwind vantage at Cojo. The secret of successful island cruising is to use your windward advantage.

NORTHBOUND PASSAGE-MAKING

Los Angeles or San Diego based yachts have a long windward passage in front of them if they plan a visit to San Miguel or even Santa Cruz island. The best plan is to motor upwind, making use of the calm hours, to take in the mainland ports of the channel on the way N, and to cross to the islands from, say, Santa Barbara, Goleta, or Refugio, or Sacate.

For example, plan to leave Marina del Rey after sunset one day, steer to pass outside Anacapa and through the passage between that island and Santa Cruz. By late morning the next day, you will be heading into Windy Lane, where you pick up a fine westerly to carry you on one tack into Santa Barbara. From Santa Barbara, you can motor sail up the coast to Refugio or Sacate, spend the night, and then cross to San Miguel. Headwinds are lighter inshore, and with correct timing, you can minimize the slogging against westerlies.

Sometimes you can use offshore breezes to your advantage. Occasionally, a light offshore or SE air can carry you up the coast close inshore at night, but such winds are not reliable. Once at Channel

Islands harbor, you can spend a full day beating from Oxnard to Santa Barbara, a far from unpleasant passage. Sometimes, you may pick up an offshore wind off the Oxnard plain early in the morning that will waft you upwind, perhaps as far as the Rincon off Carpinteria, before it dies. If you are feeling really ambitious, ride this wind up to Santa Cruz Island, spend a day there, then sail to Santa Barbara on the afternoon westerly.

In summary, use the mainland coast for windward passages, the island shores when southbound.

Your landmarks for the E entrance of the Santa Barbara Channel are:

• A conspicuous sand dune that lies 2 miles E of Point Mugu on the mainland. This is marked on Chart 18720.

• Point Mugu itself, a detached rock caused by blasting the headland for Highway 1. This will be spotted soon after the sand dune. Both these features are useful landmarks when tacking inshore from the W end of Catalina island.

• Anacapa island. The peak at the W end is conspicuous. At night Anacapa light (Gp. Fl. 3 60 sec.) is visible for 27 miles and a vital landmark. Anacapa radiobeacon (.. .. AN) is audible on 323 kHz for 10 miles.

• Ormond Beach Generating Station, 2.4 miles SE of Point Hueneme. The power plant has two conspicuous red and white smoke stacks.

THE MAINLAND COAST
(Chart 18721; *Chart Kit*, p.2; *ChartGuide, pp.D5-6*)

After Point Conception, the coast trends to the E, with lowlying yellow cliffs backed by low mountains as far as Gaviota. The Santa Ynez mountains form a spectacular backdrop to the coastal plain. US 101 and the railroad run along the coast between Gaviota and Goleta. The trestles are sometimes conspicuous. The suburbs of Santa Barbara and Goleta start at Coal Oil Point, and the campus buildings and carrillon tower of the University of California are visible from ten miles or more offshore. The cliffs are higher between the campus and Lavigia Hill, that forms the W landmark for the Santa Barbara harbor.

Extensive kelp beds line the entire coast about ¼- to ½-mile offshore.

Most yachts will sail direct from Cojo to Santa Barbara, in which case you are best advised to stay well offshore, steering about 110 deg. M until you are level with the E end of San Miguel. Then head direct for Santa Barbara. You will probably enjoy better tail winds, and will avoid the natural oil that seeps out closer inshore between Gaviota and Goleta. The oil platforms off Gaviota, Refugio, and Coal Oil Point offer good landmarks for this passage. If you decide to sail the inshore course, keep an eye out for strong gusts from the canyons behind Gaviota and Refugio. *This area is dangerous in clear, NE conditions, and should be avoided.* NW wind strengths can be predicted with the aid of veil clouds.

Photo: PETER HOWORTH

Sacate anchorage from S, distant 0.75 mile. This little known anchorage is a convenient, and sheltered mainland refuge.

The *Cruising Guide* describes a series of shelter anchorages between Conception and Santa Barbara.

• Secate (or Sacate according to the chart) lies 4.5 miles W of Gaviota, a spacious anchorage that offers superb protection from NW winds and heavy surge. It lies due N of oil platform Helen and can be identified by two conspicuous railroad embankments and Razorback Point, a prominent headland with sloping strata. Anchor off the E railroad embankment in 30 ft., sand and rock, avoiding the kelp.

• Refugio is a useful anchorage 7.5 miles E. of Gaviota pier. You can identify Refugio from the conspicuous freeway trestle behind the anchorage, and by a prominent red barn and some green buildings immediately W. Anchor inside the kelp, behind the point in 15 to 20 feet, sand. This anchorage can be bumpy. Sacate is preferable.

• Goleta Beach offers limited shelter off the University or the recently extended fishing pier in 15 to 30 feet, sand. Lay plenty of scope and beware of the sewer line W of the pier, marked with kelp.

All these anchorages are good spots for embarking on an island crossing, especially to Santa Rosa and San Miguel.

• Santa Barbara (Chart 18725, *Chart Kit*, p.7; *ChartGuide*, pp E1-2) is one of the most picturesque communities on the coast with a small and crowded harbor, remarkable for its friendly atmosphere. The approach to the town from W is straightforward, once you have recognized Lavigia Hill and the yellow cliffs of Santa Barbara Point. Santa Barbara Point light is Fl. 10 sec. and is theoretically visible for 25 miles. The harbor breakwater and Stearn's Wharf will come into view once you have Santa Barbara light abeam. Stay at least a mile offshore to avoid kelp. The E approach is even simpler, for Lavigia Hill stands out as a separate area of high ground from the Santa Ynez mountains. Steer for the N side of the hill until the buildings of Santa Barbara City College come into sight immediately above the harbor. Inbound from the islands, steer for a conspicuous grey-colored cleft in the mountains immediately above the town until the city college buildings become clear and you can identify the breakwaters.

Santa Barbara entrance is subject to constant shoaling and is dredged periodically. Two black approach buoys mark the fairway, and lead to a dredged channel that curves round to the W past a sandbar.

Photo: GRAHAM POMEROY

Santa Barbara harbor from SE, altitude 3000 feet. The sand bar can be discerned on the port side of the entrance.

Keep inside the channel, and do not steer for the sandbar. You would be surprised how many respectable skippers ground on the sand as a result of this mistake. Once inside the harbor report to the harbor director's office at the head of the harbor for a berth assignment. You can anchor off the E side of Stearn's Wharf, but the anchorage is uncomfortable and holding ground dubious. Do not try this in SE weather. You will end up on the beach. Night entrance can be difficult for a stranger. Stearn's Wharf and the breakwater are lit, but the lights are confused against the lights of the town. The channel is basically unlit, and you need to spot the buoys against the lighter color of the beach. Best anchor E of Stearn's Wharf and wait for daylight. Santa Barbara harbor is a dead lee shore in SE gales and should not be attempted under such conditions. If dredging operations are in progress, contact the harbor office on Channel 16 for information. Santa Barbara offers all reasonable facilities for small craft, but be warned that visitors' slips are in short supply in the summer months.

SANTA BARBARA TO VENTURA AND CHANNEL ISLANDS
(Chart 18725; *Chart Kit,* pp.7-8; *ChartGuide,* pp.E1-6)

Ventura Marina lies 23 miles E of Santa Barbara, and is reached by a pleasant coastal passage along a mountainous shoreline, with US 101 close inshore. You can often ride an E-bound current on this leg by staying about a mile offshore. The mountains give way to low, coastal plains at the Ventura river. The city marina lies at the point where the bight of Pierpoint Bay turns SE. **Ventura Marina** entrance (*Chart Kit* p.8; *ChartGuide* p. 4) can be identified by the two green and one silver oil storage tanks that lie behind the breakwaters. You should be able to spot the harbor breakwaters once the pier is abeam.

The Ventura entrance is protected by a detached breakwater that runs parallel to the land. You enter behind the S extremity, then steer up the dredged channel that leads between the two harbor jetties. Apply to the harbormaster's office on the point N of the entrance basin for a slip. All repair facilities, water and fuel.

Unfortunately, Ventura entrance is extremely dangerous in strong winds and heavy seas. It is also subject to shoaling. If in doubt, call the harbormaster on Channel 16, or divert elsewhere. In spite of good lights and a radiobeacon (.... _ VM) on 314 kHz, a night entrance to Ventura is inadvisable without local knowledge. Try Channel Islands instead.

The entire, low-lying coast between Ventura and Point Hueneme is a dangerous lee shore in strong W winds. Stay well clear of the beach in these conditions.

• **Channel Islands Harbor** (*Chart Kit,* p. 9; *ChartGuide,* pp. 5-6) is a pleasant, all-weather yacht harbor. You should, however, use caution when approaching the entrance in rough weather, and radio the harbormaster on Channel 16 before attempting entrance.

The approach to Channel Islands harbor from Santa Barbara or the islands is best made by identifying the Mandalay Bay Generating Plant, which can be seen from a long distance offshore. Note that it has *one* smokestack; Ormond Bay S of Point Hueneme has two. The power station is 3 miles N of Channel Islands harbor. The harbor entrance is difficult to spot, for the breakwater merges with the land. The approach from S is simplicity itself. Just follow the land round from Point Hueneme staying a mile offshore, and you will soon sight the breakwater. Like Ventura, Channel Islands harbor is protected by a stone breakwater parallel to the beach. You should enter past the S end, then turn starboard to the entrance channel between the jetties. The harbormaster's office is to starboard of the harbor basin, and transient slips can be obtained there. Channel Islands harbor has all reasonable facilities for yachts. Night entrance is easy enough provided you can identify the Fl.G. 6 sec. light on the S breakwater, which can only be seen 6 miles away. This light is easily lost against the land. However, Point Hueneme light (Fl. 5 sec. 22 miles) is prominent in most weather conditions. Channel Islands harbor radiobeacon (-... .. CI) broadcasts on 308 kHz from the S jetty, with a range of 10 miles.

In my judgement, Channel Islands is a vastly superior harbor to Ventura for a passage-making yacht. It is located close to Point Hueneme and the islands, and you can sometimes ride a land breeze up-channel to Santa Barbara or Santa Cruz Island in the mornings. The entrance is also much safer than Ventura, or even Santa Barbara.

CHANNEL ISLANDS HARBOR TO POINT DUME
(Charts 18720, 25, 40; *Chart Kit,* p.3, *ChartGuide,* pp.E6 & H1)

Channel Islands lies a mile E of Point Hueneme, a gravel and sand spit that displays an important light (Fl. 5 sec. 22 miles). The military port for the Hueneme military facilities lies immediately SE of the point and is effectively off limits for yachts. Make for Channel Islands harbor instead. From Point Hueneme to Point Mugu, the sandy floodplain is only a few feet above sea level. Ormond Beach generating plant with its two smoke stacks is conspicuous 2.4 miles SE

Photo: GRAHAM POMEROY

Channel Islands harbor from W, altitude 3000 feet. The main entrance is on the S side of the offshore breakwater.

of Port Hueneme. The air base runway extends seaward just E of the plant.

Low flying jets may pass over your head as you sail by. This part of the coastline is technically in the Pacific Missile Range. A patrolling launch may ask you to wait for a firing, a delay that will last only a few minutes. You can obtain advance information by calling "Plead Control" on Channel 16 or at (805) 982-8841 or 982-4127. If you are unable to raise Control, call Channel Islands Coast Guard, who may be able to assist. To complicate things even further, there is a small arms range just N of Point Mugu. Look for the red flags and keep at least 2 miles offshore to avoid richochets...

• Point Mugu is readily identified by two silver oil storage tanks on the peak behind the headland, conspicuous white radar domes, and by the detached rock of the point itself. S of Mugu, the coastline is steep and precipitous as far as Point Dume, 14 miles away. Highway 1 hugs the coastline, passing by the conspicuous dunes that are such a good marker for the southern approach to the Santa Barbara Channel. They are marked "Prominent Slide" on Chart 18720 and 740, and *ChartGuide*, p. H1. Except for a large condominium development some 5 miles N of Point Dume, there are few no other features on this stretch of steep coast. Point Dume is a reddish bluff about 200 feet high, with white cliffs on its E and W sides. Keep at least a mile offshore, outside the whistle buoy off the point (Fl. 4 sec.). This is usually easy to spot at night.

Decent anchorages don't exist between Point Hueneme and Point Dume. Northbound yachts can expect brisk headwinds along this stretch of coast on summer afternoons, especially N of Point Mugu, where the wind funnels between Anacapa and the mainland.

THE OFFSHORE ISLANDS

A full description of the Channel Islands will be found in the *Cruising Guide, ChartGuide*, and in the *Pacific Boating Almanac*. Here are some notes for the benefit of passage-makers, which concentrate on general navigational strategy and refuge anchorages.

San Miguel (Chart 18727; *Chart Kit*, p.10; *ChartGuide* pp.F3-4)

San Miguel is part of the Channel Islands National Park, and one of the most fascinating places I have ever visited. The island is notorious for its strong winds, and may be approached either from Cojo or Refugio, or from Santa Rosa Island. A crossing from the mainland should be made relatively early in the day. If you cross from Refugio, be prepared to allow for a pronounced W set which flows up-channel sometimes. The approach from Santa Rosa Island is best made from the S side. Leave Johnson's Lee at dawn and motor W (keeping well ashore to avoid Bee Rock), so you arrive in Cuyler Harbor before the winds fill in. On no account approach San Miguel at night, in rough weather, or with a landfall on the W end in mind. Both are potentially disastrous tactics.

The only relatively all-weather harbor is Cuyler, on the NE coast of the island. The entrance lies immediately E of Harris Point, a precipitous headland that can be identified far offshore on clear days. Steer for the headland until the entrance opens up. Then steer towards the land, favoring the San Miguel side, on a course one-third of the distance between Prince Island and the cliffs. The anchorage will appear to starboard. You can turn into the bay once you are clear of a shallow spit that runs SE from the land. Anchor well into the bight in 25 to 35 feet. Lay plenty of scope, and be prepared to clear out if swells roll around the point. Cuyler is sheltered from NW to SW winds, but is no place to be caught in a winter SE gale.

Important Note: *San Miguel is a National Park and landing (except on Cuyler beach) is prohibited except in the company of a Ranger. For an appointment, apply to the Channel Islands National Park, 1699 Anchors Way Drive, Ventura, CA 93003 (805) 644-8157.*

Santa Rosa (Charts 18727/8; *Chart Kit* pp.11-12; *ChartGuide*, pp.F5-6)

Your best course from San Miguel is to pass through the San Miguel Passage and along the S coast of Santa Rosa. If you traverse the N shore, stay at least 2 miles offshore to avoid shoals off the NW coast. Whichever side you pass, your refuge anchorages are Johnson's Lee near South Point and Northwest Anchorage in Bechers Bay at the E end of the island. Northwest is an open roadstead with a pier that provides excellent shelter from prevailing westerlies. The smoothest water and fair shelter can be found under the cliffs 0.5 mile N of the pier. Try to anchor clear of the kelp, in 30 feet, sand and rock. Sometimes heavy swells roll into the anchorage. There is 16 feet at the end of the pier.

Important Note: *Landing on Santa Rosa is by permit only, and then only at Bechers Bay. Apply to: Vail and Vickers, 123 W Padre Street, Suite D, Santa Barbara, CA 93105.*

Santa Cruz (Charts 18728/9; *Chart Kit* pp.13-14 *ChartGuide,* pp.G1-4)

Santa Cruz is the jewel of the offshore islands, unspoiled, breathtakingly beautiful, and crammed with fine anchorages. We cannot even begin to do justice to the magnificent cruising ground here. Refer to the *Cruising Guide,* chapters 7 and 8, *ChartGuide,* and the *Pacific Boating Almanac,* for full details. The passage-making yacht may use three useful refuge anchorages along the N and E coasts:

• **Fry's Harbor** lies just E of Diablo point, a conspicuous headland that rises to the highest point of land on the island. The anchorage is safe in almost any W weather. Anchor bow-in as close to the beach as you can in 30 feet, laying two anchors to guard against canyon winds.

• **Pelican Bay** is the most famous Santa Cruz anchorage, and can be identified by a low bluff with prominent tree clumps on its W side. It lies a mile W of Prisoner's Harbor, the main landing on the island. Anchor in the middle of the bay in 35 feet, sand and weed, making sure your anchor is well dug in. Pelican can be bumpy in strong winds. Fry's is preferable as a refuge.

• **Smugglers Cove** faces on Anacapa Passage, a large, open roadstead that provides shelter against W winds. Strong down canyon winds can blow through this anchorage. Anchor in 25 to 40 feet, sand, off the beach. The best shelter is under the cliffs on the NW side. This anchorage is dangerous in SE gales.

On no account anchor at Santa Cruz during dry, NE wind conditions. The anchorages become untenable, even in a moderate Santa Ana. Go to sea and stay there.

Important Note: *Landing on Santa Cruz is by permit only, a restriction that is strictly enforced. For the western portions of the island (Chinese Harbor to Sandstone Point) apply to: Santa Cruz Island Company, 515 S. Flower Street, Los Angeles, CA 90071, (213) 485-4208. A modest fee is charged. This portion of the island is now coming under The Nature Conservancy's jurisdiction. Eastern areas: Mr. Francis Gherini, 162 South A Street, Oxnard, CA 93030,(805) 483-8022. DO NOT LAND WITHOUT A PERMIT IN HAND.*

Pelican Bay, Santa Cruz Island from NNW, altitude 2000 feet. The yacht to starboard is anchored in the best position.

Anacapa Island (Chart 18729; *Chart Kit* p.15, *ChartGuide*, pp.G5-6)

Anacapa is a distinctive island with a prominent peak at its E end. No refuge anchorages exist in its shores. Its most important landmark, the lighthouse at the E end (Gp. Fl.3 60 sec.), with a light visible for 26 miles, was sketched by the young James Whistler in 1854. Give its shores a wide berth, especially in windy weather and NE conditions.

James Whistler's sketch of the E end of Anacapa Island, executed in 1854.

Photo: GRAHAM POMEROY

The E end of Anacapa from SE a century and a quarter later, showing the lighthouse.

Santa Barbara Island
(Chart 18756; *Chart Kit* p.10; *ChartGuide*, pp.G7-8)

This tiny island, 1.5 miles long, lies 40 miles SE of Santa Cruz Island. The National Park is well worth a visit in settled weather, but the island offers no secure refuge anchorage in a gale. For details, consult the *Cruising Guide*, chapter 14, *ChartGuide*, or *Pacific Boating Almanac*. You are unlikely to pass near it, or San Nicolas Island, unless you plan a special visit to these two offshore islands. In fact, I flatly recommend that you avoid San Nicolas altogether.

Important Note: *Both Anacapa and Santa Barbara islands are part of the Channel Islands National Park. For information, apply to the National Park Service office in Ventura. Passages to and from the offlying islands will require monitoring of the Pacific Missile Range (see under mainland passages above).*

Photo: JEFF BARNHART, PHOTOGRAPHY EDITOR, *DAILY NEXUS*

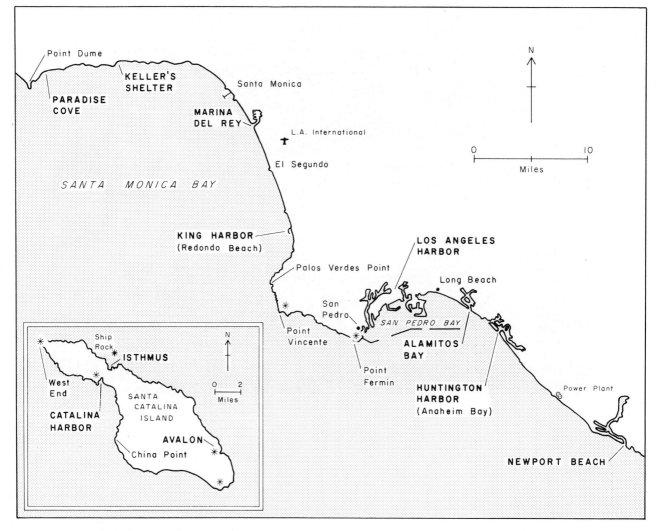

Passage chart: Point Dume to Newport Beach and Catalina Island. San Clemente Island omitted for clarity.

Point Dume to Newport Beach and Offshore Islands

SUMMARY OF PASSAGE STRATEGIES

Southbound non-stop from the Santa Barbara Channel to San Diego or Mexico, you are best advised to steer a rhumb line course, passing close to the NE coast of Catalina Island. This enables you to stop at the Isthmus or Avalon if you so desire, and to schedule your passage for the windy hours of the day. Northbound vessels are best advised to take a similar course, thereby avoiding the shipping and congestion off San Pedro.

Bound for Santa Monica Bay, San Pedro, or ports before Newport Beach, ride the winds funnelling on either side of Anacapa Island, then stay two to four miles off Point Dume before heading towards the harbor of your destination.

Navigation within the Los Angeles area is straightforward, and requires no special planning. However, you should plan on motoring north past Point Dume during the calm hours, shaping a course to pass outside Anacapa island if bound for the islands.

Hazards

Shipping constitutes a major hazard in the Los Angeles area. The main shipping lanes pass inside Catalina through well defined traffic lanes, which you should be at pains to avoid.

Santa Ana winds can create dangerous conditions off Southern California. If you plan a voyage during a Santa Ana, exercise extreme caution, and avoid the NE coast of Catalina Island at all costs.

The Pacific Missile Range straddles the area between San Nicolas Island and Point Mugu. While the area is patrolled by aircraft and boats, you should check with the Range Officer for firing times in advance.

The entrance channels of Los Angeles area harbors can be very congested at weekends. The first time visitor is advised to enter on a weekday, and to use the engine.

Oil drilling operations are conducted off Long Beach. You should give oil islands and drilling platforms a wide berth, also obvious military operations, and yacht races off the major harbors, especially at weekends or on Wednesday evenings during the summer.

Passage Times

Assuming an average of 5 knots, you can sail between Channel Islands and Marina del Rey in about 9 hours. The northbound passage will take longer, depending on wind and sea conditions. The voyage between the same port and the Isthmus takes about 12 hours under normal conditions, and considerably longer northbound, assuming you motor in the morning, then tack inshore in the afternoon, making a landfall on Point Mugu. Most destinations within the Los Angeles area can be reached in an easy day sail.

"The land was of a clayey consistency, and, as far as the eye could reach, entirely bare of trees and even shrubs; and there was no sign of a town — not even a house to be seen... We lay exposed to every wind that could blow, except the north-west, and that came over a flat country with a range of more than a league of water." Richard Henry Dana spent weeks on end anchored in San Pedro Bay. The nearest town was Pueblo de Los Angeles, about 20 miles in the interior. The crew of the *Pilgrim* would not recognize their anchorage today, for it now lies off one of the largest commercial harbors in the United States. The desolate coastline of yesteryear is now a major cruising ground for thousands of enthusiastic sailors. The ingenious people who estimate such things tell us that there is a greater concentration of sailing yachts between Marina del Rey and Newport Beach than anywhere else in the world except perhaps Southern Florida. You are in a land of vast marinas and urban sprawl, of generally quiet sailing conditions, and one where traffic jams are common in harbor entrances and highly competitive sailing is a way of life.

SOURCES OF DETAILED CRUISING INFORMATION

Our sailing directions for this crowded and fascinating area are not meant as a comprehensive guide to the fine marinas and artificial harbors that await the weekend sailor. Rather, our concern is to identify key landmarks, major harbors of refuge, and general strategies that you should bear in mind when planning a cruise along the mainland or around Catalina.

The following sources are invaluable guides to the major harbors and anchorages S of Point Dume:

• *ChartGuide for Southern California,* is especially useful because of its enlarged charts and excellent harbor plans. The charts contain a mass of information for divers and fishing boats, revised every one or two years. Brief sailing directions add to the usefulness of this publication: *ChartGuide for Catalina Island* contains all Catalina pages, from the Southern California book.

• *Pacific Boating Almanac, Southern California, Arizona, and Baja.* This annual publication contains invaluable data on harbors and facilities, also tide tables and other annual information.

• *The Southern California Chart-Kit* contains the NOS charts for this area; for your convenience, we cross-reference to both *Chart-Kit* and *ChartGuide.*

Sailing directions that follow should be combined with one or more of these admirable publications when you are past the planning stage.

GENERAL PASSAGE-MAKING INFORMATION
(Chart 18740; *Chart Kit,* p.4; *ChartGuide,* pp.H1-2 & M1-2)

The yacht bound for San Diego or Mexican waters from N of Point Dume is advised to head well offshore, and to pass close to the NE coastline of Catalina Island. You will then escape the worst of the commercial ship traffic bound to and from San Pedro and Long Beach and cross the two traffic separation schemes by short and direct routes. A more inshore course will take you through the middle of the shipping lanes, which is technically illegal. Best to enjoy the scenery of Catalina, and to approach the mainland at your southern destination rather than to skirt the coast.

If bound from the Santa Barbara Channel to Marina del Rey, or a port N of Oceanside, you will probably choose a more inshore course, in which case you must pass inside the traffic separation scheme that leads from the Anacapa Passage into San Pedro Bay. A good route takes you close inshore at Points Vincente and Fermin, and then down to Newport Beach across the Los Angeles Pilot Area. This can be a tricky passage in thick weather, especially off the great harbor breakwaters E of Point Fermin. Keep a good lookout and remember that you are sailing in restricted waters under international law. I always enjoy this sail on a fine afternoon, when the sea sparkles and the great metropolitan bustle to port seems to be another world.

A yacht sailing N from San Diego should pass close NE of Catalina, then stay well offshore until N of Point Dume. This part of the journey is best made at night, and under power. As the wind fills in, tack inshore, pick up the conspicuous sand dunes S of Point Dume, and enjoy a lusty windward passage to Channel Islands Harbor.

The northbound passage from the Los Angeles mainland to the Santa Barbara Channel is best executed at night. You may be lucky enough to pick up a Santa Ana or offshore breeze in the small hours, but assume you will have to motor. I always pass outside Anacapa island, then motor through the Anacapa Passage to pick up the westerlies in Windy Lane for the crossing to the mainland.

General Warning: *avoid longer passages in Santa Ana conditions. Dangerous gusts and steep wind waves can create havoc aboard. Catalina island in particular should be avoided, for its best anchorages and Avalon harbor are very dangerous in Santa Anas.*

POINT DUME TO MARINA DEL REY
(Chart 18744; *Chart Kit,* p.16-17; *ChartGuide* pp.H3-4)

The Santa Monica mountains form a fine backdrop to the 16 miles of E-trending coast between Point Dume and the city after which they are named. The shoreline consists of steep cliffs and stretches of beach that lead to the foothills. Heavily travelled Highway 1 runs just inshore of the cliffs. In all likelihood you will stay well outside the bight of Santa Monica Bay as you steer for Marina del Rey or King Harbor (Redondo Beach). It's wise to stay offshore in any case, for a gentle S-flowing current induces a slow, counterclockwise eddy inshore.

Two useful anchorages provide excellent temporary shelter when N-bound and waiting for calm conditions beyond Point Dume:

• **Paradise Cove** lies 2 miles NE of Point Dume. It is easily recognized by counting the arroyos E of Point Dume. The best anchorage is opposite the fourth break in the cliffs, with Point Dume bearing about 225 degrees M. You will find about 30 to 35 feet, sand, outside the kelp. Anchor in a kelp-free spot and watch out for the mooring buoys off the pier.

• **Kellers Shelter** offers some protection from N and W, 9 miles W of Santa Monica at Malibu. You can spot the 700-foot fishing pier from far off by the white buildings on its extremity. Anchor clear of the moorings in 15 to 35 feet, sand. Keep ¾-mile offshore if approaching from W, to avoid a reef marked by kelp close inshore. I prefer Paradise; Kellers is noisy from the constant traffic on Highway 1.

• **Santa Monica** is easily identified by the highrise buildings crowding down to the sea. The city pier is protected by a stone breakwater that runs parallel to the shore. You will find about 22 feet at the end of the pier, and many small craft on moorings inside the breakwater. This is an uncomfortable place; far better to proceed to Marina del Rey, 3.5 miles E, where you can berth in complete shelter. If you must anchor, you must obtain permission from (213) 451-4375 first.

Marina del Rey north entrance, distant 0.5 mile.

Photo: JASON HAILEY

MARINA DEL REY
(Chart 18744; *Chart Kit*, p.19 *ChartGuide*, pp.H5-6)

Marina del Rey is the largest man-made yacht harbor in the world, and literally defies description. To enter the marina during the weekend rush-hour is an ordeal, which I cannot recommend to a complete stranger. Plan to enter on a weekday if you can.

General Warning: *yacht racing is commonplace S of Point Dume. Keep a sharp lookout for racing marks and avoid tangling with races in progress, especially off the major harbors.*

The general area of the entrance is clearly identified, for the takeoff path of Los Angeles International Airport lies immediately SE. Huge 747s and DC 10s rush out at you over a low ridge. A tract of barren land matches the flight path. From W, identify Venice pier, with its characteristic rounded end. Marina del Rey breakwater is a mile E. A northbound vessel should identify bell buoy "2ES" (Fl. 4 sec.) which lies 3.1 miles, 344 degrees M from the breakwater. You will often find tankers moored close inshore from this buoy. In thick weather, you may confuse Ballona Creek jetty SE of the breakwaters with Marina del Rey, so approach with caution. A night arrival can be confused by the city lights, but you should identify aircraft from LA airport, and then be able to pick up the harbor lights, the most conspicuous of which is light "3" (Fl. 5 sec.) on the N jetty, visible for 15 miles. Both ends of the outer breakwater are lit by flashing lights visible for 9 miles.

Most yachts use the N entrance of Marina del Rey, as the S channel has shoaled. Strangers should plan on the N entrance, especially if they draw more than 6 feet.

Marina del Rey has traffic zoning. The traffic lanes inside jetties are marked by unlighted buoys. You MUST leave these to port and pass along the outer edges of the entrance channel if you are under power. The center lane is reserved for vessels under sail alone. If you own a larger vessel, *I strongly advise you NOT to sail into Marina del Rey.* Leave your purism behind and be considerate of others.

• No anchoring, or delaying in the entrance channel is allowed.

• Speed limits of 8 knots in the entrance, 5 elsewhere are enforced.

Once inside the marina, you will find the harbormaster's office on the starboard side. It is advisable to radio ahead on Channel 16, then 12 or 73, or to telephone (213) 823-4571 for reservations. Transient berths can sometimes be arranged with local yacht clubs and private marinas. The visitors' berths are in Basin H, to starboard in the first marina area. Stays over 7 nights are difficult to arrange.

Marina del Rey contains every conceivable facility you can possibly want, and hundreds of unique and fascinating yachts.

KING HARBOR (REDONDO BEACH)
(Chart 18744; *Chart Kit,* pp.18-19; *ChartGuide,* p.J3)

The coast between Marina del Rey and King Harbor is low-lying and heavily built up. Keep clear of offshore oil facilities and sewer outfall off El Segundo. Pass at least 1.5 miles offshore and plan to round buoy "2ES" on your way N or S. Manhattan Beach and Hermosa Beach piers are conspicuous. King Harbor is a small and pleasant haven that provides the finish for the annual Santa Barbara-King Harbor race every August. The harbor is easy to to find. Steer for the eight smokestacks of the power plant at the N end of the harbor. The northernmost stack is well marked on the chart.

King Harbor breakwater curves around parallel to the beach to protect the marinas. Enter at the SE end, which is lit (Fl. 6 sec. 12 miles). The radiobeacon (... .... RB) broadcasts on 319 kHz. A yacht drawing 6 feet can safely pass between the approach buoy and the breakwater when approaching from NW. The entrance channel inside the breakwater is marked by buoys. The marinas lie to starboard. Report to the harbormaster's office, clearly marked at the entrance to Basin 2, for a transient slip. I have always found King Harbor Yacht Club a pleasant and hospitable place. All facilities for yachts, including a boatyard.

Los Angeles light.

Photo: TONI ABBOTT

KING HARBOR TO LOS ANGELES HARBOR
(Charts 18744, 46, 49; *Chart Kit,* p.4, 18-19; *ChartGuide,* pp.J2-5)

A course of 196 degrees M will take you 4.6 miles from King Harbor entrance to red whistle buoy "10" (Fl.R 4 sec.), which lies 0.7 mile W of Point Palos Verdes. Pass outside this marker to avoid the reefs and kelp inshore. The point is bold and conspicuous, easy to distinguish from Point Vincente 2 miles SSE, the latter a reddish/white, 120 foot cliff with its 67-foot cylindrical light tower and radio antennas. Point Vincente light is a major landmark (Gp. Fl 2 20 sec. 24 miles), as is

Point Fermin (Fl. 10 sec. 16 miles) 6.3 miles SE. These two lights will bring you into the vicinity of Los Angeles harbor at night.

The coastline between Points Vincente and Fermin is rocky, and dominated by the buildings of Marineland Oceanarium 0.7 mile SE of the former headland. The white observation tower is especially conspicuous, as are white radar domes on Point Fermin. The shore is clear of outlying dangers. Keep outside the kelp and the whistle buoy and enjoy the scenery.

It is worth noting that ESE flowing currents move over the shelf off the Palos Verdes peninsula in spring and summer. They change to NW and WSW during the winter, flowing with a velocity of about 0.25 knots throughout the year.

SAN PEDRO BAY

(Charts 18749, 51; *Chart Kit,* pp.21, 26-27; *ChartGuide,* pp.J5-K6).

It was Vancouver who named Point Fermin after the then father president of the Franciscan order. Winds were too light for him to anchor in San Pedro Bay, which he observed "appeared to retire to the north-westward, probably affording anchorage and shelter." How right he was! The vast breakwaters of Los Angeles Harbor now protect this once desolate bay from all weather, forming one of the major commercial ports of the West Coast.

• **Los Angeles-Long Beach harbor** is a commercial haven. Small craft may enter the harbor, but must always be aware they must give way to ships operating in these restricted waters. A Precautionary Area off the harbor is clearly marked on the charts. Exercise extreme caution in operating in this area, as it is often congested with incoming and outgoing ships. *Be especially careful to keep clear of the ends of the Traffic Lanes off Point Fermin and close to buoy "3TL" (Fl. 3 sec.), 5 miles from the breakwaters.*

The outer harbor is protected by breakwaters that extend about 4 miles E from Point Fermin. You can enter the outer harbor through either the W or Long Beach channel entrances, or pass around the E

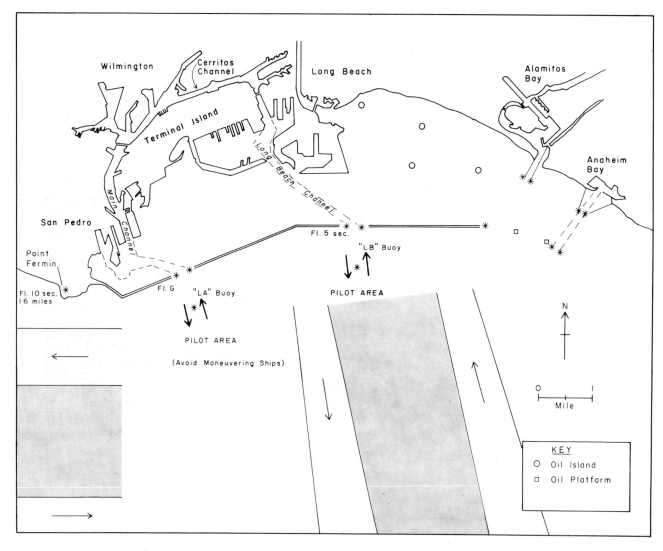

San Pedro Bay: general plan. Warning: this plan should not be used for navigation. Use NOS charts.

Photo: AERIAL EYE, INC., IRVINE, CALIFORNIA.

San Pedro Bay from SW.

"This bay is well protected in every direction, except against the winter gales from the southeast round to the southwest. During the spring, summer, and winter, it is an excellent roadstead...Vessels must anchor a mile off to get five fathoms...In winter anchor further out, and more to the southward, in order to be able to slip the cable and go to sea should a strong southeaster spring up...Wood and water are not readily obtained, and the charges are high. The beef raised here is remarkably tough."
—*GEORGE DAVIDSON, 1858*

end of Long Beach breakwater. Keep a sharp lookout for commercial traffic entering and leaving the harbor. Do not be tempted to go up close to a big ship "to have a look." I once heard a Long Beach pilot lecture about his job. "Keep clear," he said firmly. "We don't have the room to get out of the way if you cross our bows."

San Pedro outer harbor is easy to find at night. The entrances are lit:

• Los Angeles light (Fl. G 15 sec.) marks the W entrance. It is exhibited from a 69-foot high cylindrical tower with vertical black stripes. You can see it 22 miles away. The radiobeacon (.. A) broadcasts on 302 kHz.

• Long Beach light (Fl. 5 sec. 24 miles) marks the Long Beach channel entrance. It shines from a white skeleton tower and broadcasts a radiobeacon on 296 kHz (.... .... LB).

• The light marking the E extremity of the Long Beach breakwater is fainter (Fl. 6 sec. 9 miles).

If *entering* the Long Beach channel entrance, you are required to keep E of black and white buoy "LB", if *leaving,* keep W.

I am ambivalent about San Pedro Bay. It is fun to see the commercial shipping and industrial activity and to sail close to the *Queen Mary* in Long Beach harbor. This is not a place for a visitor to dawdle, however. Perhaps your best bet is to make a diversion through the breakwaters, explore the outer harbor, and then make for Alamitos Bay or Newport for the night. Bureaucratic regulations governing San Pedro fill page after page of the *Pilot.* While most of these affect large vessels, you should peruse them carefully and be sure to have Charts 18749, 51, 52 on board. The *ChartGuide for Southern California* is especially helpful, for it provides overprinted information of yachting facilities on pages J5-K4.

The *ChartGuide* also provides summary information on small boat facilities:

• **San Pedro**: see *ChartGuide,* p.J5. East and West channels: Contact Holiday Harbor (213) 833-4468, Cabrillo Boat Shop (213) 832-2609; or California Yacht Anchorage (213) 833-2492. Al Larsen Marine (213) 832-0526 and Los Angeles Yacht Club (213) 833-2492 in the Fish

Harbor are possible berths E of the Main channel. Be sure to call in good time.

• **Inner Harbor**: see *ChartGuide*, p.J7. A variety of marinas lie off the Los Angeles Main channel and Cerritos channel, most of them concentrated on either side of the Henry Ford and Heim Bridges.

• **Long Beach**: see *ChartGuide*, pp. K1-4 marinas are under construction. You can try Lands End Marina (213) 437-0191 or West 7th Street slips (213) 432-5062.

ALAMITOS BAY (LONG BEACH MARINA)
(Chart 18749; *Chart Kit*, p.28; *ChartGuide*, p.K4.)

By far the best yacht harbor for visitors is Alamitos Bay, on the E side of San Pedro Bay. The entrance lies a mile NE of the E end of the Long Beach breakwater and is easy to locate from all directions. The two jetties protecting the entrance channel are lit, so a night approach is straightforward. A row of buoys down the center of the channel (17 feet) delineate traffic lanes: you leave the buoys to port.

The harbor director's office is on the starboard side of the entrance (213) 498-1391, and transient slips are available. You may occupy one for a maximum of 15 days in a 30-day period. All yacht facilities are available. This is a pleasant and quiet harbor.

• **Huntington Harbor,** a mile SE of Alamitos Bay, is a private development, accessible through Anaheim Bay harbor, the site of the US Naval Weapons Station. State-registered and documented vessels may enter *under power* at a speed not exceeding 5 knots, subject to special military controls. The yacht harbor mainly consists of private homes with docks, and is accessible under a bridge with 22-foot clearance. There are some transit slips, but the visitor is probably best advised to go to Alamitos Bay.

It is possible to confuse Anaheim Bay lights for those of Alamitos when making a night approach. Confusion is easy to avoid if you remember that the latter has red and green flashing entrance lights. Explosives are sometimes moved in Anaheim Bay. At that time you may be subject to movement controls.

ANAHEIM BAY TO NEWPORT BEACH
(Chart 18746; *Chart Kit*, pp. 29-30; *ChartGuide*, pp.J4, M2)

The 14 miles of coast between Anaheim Bay and Newport Beach are low-lying and sandy. A continuous ribbon of urban development backs the beach. The two smokestacks of the Southern California Edison plant 5.5 miles NW of Newport entrance provide an admirable land- mark even far offshore. You are best advised to keep outside the 10-fathom line along this stretch of coast to avoid mooring buoys and other industrial paraphernalia. Oil rigs off the E end of San Pedro Bay are also prominent.

NEWPORT BEACH
(Chart 18754; *Chart Kit*, p. 30; *ChartGuide*, pp.Q3-6)

No cruise in Southern California is complete without a visit to this fine harbor. The approach from NW should first identify the two smoke stacks of the power plant, then the highrise buildings of the Newport Center, 1.4 miles N of the harbor. Once within a mile of shore you should see the twin jetties of the entrance, marked by bell buoy "I" (Fl.G 4 sec.) just offshore. The northbound skipper will prob- ably see the breakwaters projecting from the low shoreline and the Newport Center highrises from a considerable distance. From Catalina, your first landmarks will be the highrises and the power plant, then bell buoy "4", 3.8 miles 080 degrees M from the jetties.

Entering Newport, keep to starboard bound in either direction. The entrance channel carries 18 feet at its deepest part, and is buoyed. Night entrance is easy, once you identify the Fl. 5 sec light on the westerly breakwater. A radiobeacon (-. . NE) broadcasts on 285 kHz. Be sure to keep in the dredged channel, especially in busy traffic periods. I have actually been forced aground when inbound at Sunday afternoon cocktail time. The first time visitor is best advised to plan a weekday arrival to avoid congestion. The many channels and marinas are well displayed in the *ChartGuide*. You should use this publication to navigate in the harbor.

Visiting yachts should report to the harbor office (714) 834-2654, which lies on the NE side of the main channel, just below the Balboa Yacht Club. They have some temporary slips and moorings. You can also try one of the local yacht clubs or private marinas mentioned in the *ChartGuide*. But be warned that Newport is very busy and temporary berths are in short supply.

Perhaps it is best to anchor in one of the designated areas (C1 to C3) shown in the *ChartGuide*. You must move if the harbor patrol tell you, and display anchor lights. Talk to the harbor office before anchoring in these areas. They all suffer from constant wash from passing vessels, a major problem in Newport Beach.

Newport has every imaginable facility, and is a marvelous place to explore in a small sailing dinghy. If you don't own one, try renting a sailboat for a few hours. You'll acquire a unique perspective on these sheltered waters.

This is a convenient place to use as a departure point for a cruise to Catalina island, between 26 and 30 miles offshore. Newport is comfortable in all weather, but you should use caution In Santa Ana conditions, when NE winds of great velocity can blow across the coast and through the entrance. Stay well offshore in this weather.

SANTA CATALINA ISLAND
(Charts 18757, 59; *Chart Kit,* pp.22-25; *ChartGuide,* pp.M1-N6)

Catalina was visited by Juan Cabrillo in 1542, and named La Victoria. Sebastian Vizcaino anchored in a "very good cove" in 1602 on St Catherine's Day, whence Santa Catalina. He found the island densely populated by friendly Indians who took "everything unguarded." Two hundred and fifty years later, George Davidson was to write that the people were "reported to be very ingenious, particularly in pilfering and concealing; some examples of the accomplishments they gave the Spaniards." Today, 86 percent of the island is owned by the Santa Catalina Island Conservancy, a charitable foundation designed to preserve animals, plants, and open land. The remainder is in the hands of the Santa Catalina Island Company.

From the point of view of the passage-making yacht, Catalina is a splendid convenience and rest stop. You can find comprehensive details of Catalina anchorages, ports, and coves in the *ChartGuide for Southern California*. Relevant sections can be purchased separately as the *ChartGuide for Catalina Island*. The *Pacific Boating Almanac* and the *Cruising Guide to the Channel Islands* also cover Catalina in considerable detail. You should have at least one of these volumes on board if you plan a cruise to and from Catalina, or around its shores. The sailing directions that follow are concerned more with cruise planning and short stays than they are with specific Catalina cruises.

Approaches To Catalina

Southbound, you will usually approach Catalina from NNW, from Channel Islands harbor or Anacapa. Try to make this passage by day, for the steep, sloping cliffs of West End will be sighted from a considerable distance. West End light (Fl. 6 sec. 7 miles) is far too faint to be an effective landmark. I remember running down on the island at twilight on a first visit. It was blowing 35 knots from astern. We rushed on in the gathering darkness and cloud and were only a mile off the land when the pin prick of the light suddenly appeared.

The best course S to San Diego takes you along the NE coast, which gives you a choice of two admirable refuge places:

• **Isthmus Cove** (Chart 18759; *Chart Kit*, pp. 23-24; *ChartGuide*, pp. M1-8) 6 miles SE of West End, provides shelter in prevailing W and NW conditions. You can identify the Isthmus area from a long way offshore because of the low topography, for a narrow spit of land joins the E and W portions of the island. In the entrance Ship Rock is conspicuous, a "haystack with a white summit," as the *Pilot* puts it. Ship Rock is lit (Fl. 4 sec. 6 miles). Your best approach is to steer for Ship Rock, then enter the cove well to the W of Bird Rock, a rounded, white-topped outcrop 150 yards long SE of Ship Rock. Give this, and Harbor Reefs, S of the rock, a wide berth.

The harbormaster's office at the foot of the pier will allocate you a vacant mooring or direct you to anchorage. Otherwise anchor outside the moorings in 60 feet, sand. No anchor lights are required. Lay two anchors to reduce the motion.

Avalon harbor approach from NNE, distant 1.5 miles. The circular casino building is to starboard of the entrance.

One major problem with Catalina is that the best coves are congested with privately owned moorings. In many cases you will have to pick up a mooring or anchor in very deep and exposed water.

• **Avalon harbor** (Chart 18759; *Chart Kit*, p.25; *ChartGuide*, pp. N5-6) is a popular port of call at the SE corner of Catalina. The southbound yacht should identify Ship Rock and the Isthmus, then Long Point (Fl. 2½ sec. 6 miles) and the KBIG Radio tower on Blackjack Peak midway between Long Point and Avalon. The station's AM signal on 740 kHz is a useful signpost on thick days. The port of Avalon will open up on the starboard bow, with the famous circular casino building conspicuous.

Harbor breakwaters project from each side of Avalon Bay, and you should enter midway between them. Keep a sharp lookout for seaplane traffic. Avalon harbor is lit by flashing white and red lights. A radiobeacon (.- .... AV) broadcasts from Casino Point on 307 kHz.

The harbormaster (213) 831-8822 and Channel 16, then 12, allocates moorings when they are available. A harbor boat will meet you and escort you to a mooring. A word of warning: Avalon is extremely crowded in summer months, and you are best advised to lie over elsewhere if you want to be sure of a berth and are weary

The northbound yacht will approach Catalina from SE, after a fairly long passage from the mainland. Your key landmark is the circular casino building and others on the W side of Avalon. This cluster of buildings is the major concentration of structures on the island and is unmistakable. The Wrigley Mansion, high above the E side of the harbor, is a useful landmark when floodlit at night. You can then make for the harbor or pass up the NW coast to the Isthmus.

The mainland crossing presents no special problems, *provided* you keep a sharp lookout for commercial traffic and cross the Traffic Separation Zones by the shortest route possible. Do not approach them in thick weather. It could be suicide. Bound from, say Marina del Rey, to the Isthmus, simply steer for the low shoulder of land that separates the E and W portions of the island until you pick up Ship Rock and other landmarks. Bound for Avalon from the mainland, you should steer just E of the highest peaks on the island, which lie W of Avalon. You can normally pick up the buildings of the town far offshore. The flashing red light of the KBIG radio tower on Blackjack Peak is prominent at night. You will experience a variety of currents in the San Pedro Channel. Daily currents operate in a rotary fashion, setting N at 0900, E at 1500, S at 2100, and W at 0300, with a velocity of 0.2 knot. A southerly, inshore current runs near the mainland at between 0.25 to 1 knot during fall and winter.

Most passage-making yachts will stay on the NE coast of Catalina, unless choosing to visit Catalina Harbor, 7 miles SE of West End. Catalina Harbor offers excellent protection in prevailing westerly conditions, and forms the other half of the Isthmus. Bound from NW, identify Eagle Rock, a detached outcrop 0.4 mile S of West End light. Then follow the coast SE 6.5 miles to the deep indentation that forms the entrance to Catalina Harbor. Structures and moorings inside the harbor will appear as you open up the entrance between the two rocky headlands. A yacht approaching from SE should follow the kelp beds rounding China Point, then identify the indentation that marks the entrance. Catalina Harbor light (Fl. 4 sec. 11 miles) is obscured through 104 to 208 degrees, and shows a higher intensity beam on 030 degrees.

You can anchor outside the moorings in Catalina Harbor in 24 to 30 feet mud and sand. A second anchor is advisable astern to minimize swinging. Keep clear of the seaplane landing area. This is an excellent anchorage from which to depart for Santa Barbara Island, 20 miles from West End.

For detailed information on Catalina, consult the sources given above.

Important Note: *Landing cards are required to land on privately owned parts of the island, except Avalon. This includes both the Isthmus and Catalina Harbor. Apply to: Catalina Cove and Camp Agency at Isthmus Cove or to PO Box 1566, Avalon, CA 90704 (213) 832-4531. $35 a year or $2.50 per adult per day (1980).*

SAN CLEMENTE ISLAND
(Charts 18762-4; *Chart Kit* pp.38-39; *ChartGuide,* pp.P1-4)

San Clemente has been owned by the Federal Government since 1848 and is off limits to the public. It lies 43 miles SSW of Point Fermin and 19 miles beyond Catalina. From a distance it looks like a table mountain, with the NE coast being particularly bold and conspicuous. A large, white radar dome can be seen on the highest point of the island from a long distance. The SW shore is more irregular and has more gentle topography. Much of the island is masked by dense kelp beds, making it a fishing paradise. George Davidson had little to say for San Clemente: "Very few trees were found, and the aspect is sterile," he wrote.

There seems little point in making the long passage out to San Clemente unless you can land, which you cannot. You may pass close by on your way far offshore, in which case you will identify the island lights, visible for about 6 miles. Wilson Cove and Northwest harbor are used by the military, and subject to restricted access. For full details, consult the *Cruising Guide to the Channel Islands* or *ChartGuide for Southern California,* pp. P1-2.

For information on restricted anchorages and island regulations, contact The Commander, Amphibious Force, Pacific Fleet, Naval Amphibious Base, Coronado (714) 437-2231.

Unless you like fishing, I would advise leaving San Clemente Island to the day when public access is restored. There are just as attractive anchorages closer to home. Most coastal passage-makers will pass far inshore.

General Warning: *Catalina is extremely dangerous in Santa Ana conditions, especially between November and March. Avalon, the Isthmus and Catalina Harbor are dangerous in such conditions. Santa Anas of up to 70 knots have been recorded at Catalina Harbor. IF SUCH CONDITIONS ARE FORECAST, LEAVE AT ONCE. It is best to stay in open water, but you can try and shelter off the NW coast, or in a cove with some protection from NE. IF IN DOUBT, HEAVE TO AT SEA WELL CLEAR OF COMMERCIAL TRAFFIC AND LEE SHORES.*

Avalon harbor during Santa Ana conditions.

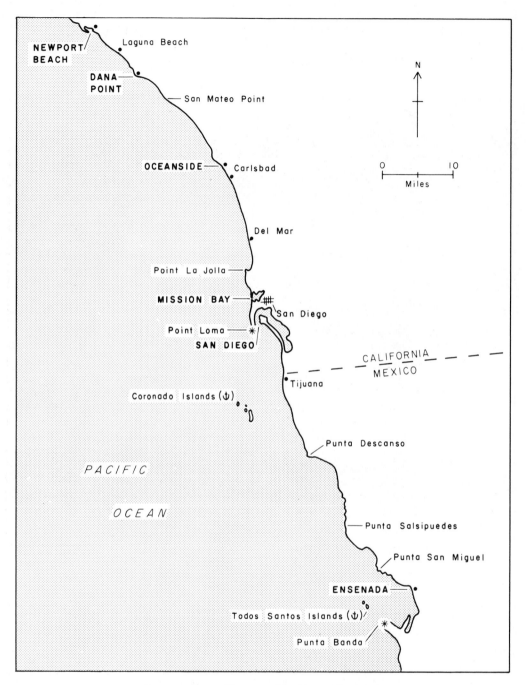

NEWPORT
BEACH

Laguna Beach

DANA
POINT

San Mateo Point

OCEANSIDE — Carlsbad

Del Mar

Point La Jolla

MISSION BAY

San Diego

Point Loma

SAN DIEGO

CALIFORNIA
MEXICO

Tijuana

Coronado Islands (⚓)

Punta Descanso

PACIFIC

OCEAN

Punta Salsipuedes

Punta San Miguel

ENSENADA

Todos Santos Islands (⚓)

Punta Banda

N

0   10
Miles

Passage chart: Newport Beach to Ensenada.

Newport Beach to Ensenada, Mexico

CHAPTER 8

SUMMARY OF PASSAGE STRATEGIES

The passage from Newport Beach to San Diego or Ensenada involves deciding whether you prefer to sail close to the beach, or further offshore. Most yachts stay offshore, passing outside the Coronados on their way to Ensenada. The northbound passage is best taken under power, staying inshore in the hopes you will pick up some form of land breeze during the night.

Yachts bound from Ensenada to San Diego normally pass inside the islands and make the passage during the calm night hours. The journey from San Diego to Catalina is a comfortable overnight motor, or a long day sail southbound, which will keep you well clear of inshore traffic.

Hazards

Commercial shipping approaches San Pedro though this area, and you should avoid main shipping lanes, also Naval ships operating off San Diego entrance.

Santa Ana winds can be a major hazard, especially in the fall. You should avoid the NE coast of Catalina Island under these conditions.

Dana Point and Mission Bay can present somewhat of a hazard in strong SE gales, or heavy swells. You are best advised to make for San Diego or Oceanside in rough weather.

The coastline between La Jolla and Point Loma is protected by thick kelp beds. Stay well offshore in this vicinity.

Passage Times

Assuming an average of 5 knots, you will take about 15 hours to sail from Avalon to San Diego, and the inside of a day to reach Oceanside from Newport Beach. Newport to Ensenada can be accomplished in about 15 hours under sail, but the passage back will take you much longer. If you leave San Diego in the morning, you can be in Ensenada by early evening under normal conditions.

The start of the 1975 Newport-Ensenada Yacht Race. This spectacular aerial view shows the Newport Harbor breakwaters and the conspicuous highrise buildings above the town that serve as a useful landmark from offshore.

Our first port is Dana Point, named after Richard Henry himself: "San Juan is the only romantic spot in California. The country here for several miles is high table-land, running boldly to the shore, and breaking off in a steep hill, at the foot of which the waters of the Pacific are constantly dashing... Just where we landed was a small cove, or "bight," which gave us, at high tide, a few square feet of sand-beach between the sea and the bottom of the hill. This was the only landing place. Directly before us, rose the perpendicular height of four or five hundred feet...There was a grandeur in everything around, which gave almost a solemnity to the scene; a silence and solitariness which affected everything. Not a human being but ourselves for miles; and no sound heard but the pulsations of the great Pacific. And the great steep hill rising like a wall and us from all the world, but the "world of waters." Dana would not recognize his favorite cliff today, the first major coastal landmark S of Newport Beach. The snug cove has gone and is replaced by acres of land fill and a fine yacht harbor. He would be flattered to know that Dana Point is named after him. But to discover a similar solitude and romance you must sail to the unspoiled coves of the offshore islands, where life is still much as it was in the 1830s.

GENERAL PASSAGE-MAKING OBSERVATIONS

Yachts bound between Catalina and San Diego or further afield are best advised to stay close to the rhumb line, and well offshore, skirting the Catalina coast. Southbound from Newport Beach to Ensenada, you have to decide whether to skirt the beach or follow an offshore course. In either case, the voyage is going to involve a night passage when the wind may drop on you. Opinion is almost equally divided between those who advocate going offshore and those who like the breakers at Ensenada Race time. A cruising yacht is probably best advised to lay a course offshore, which takes you either just outside or immediately inshore of the Coronado islands SW of San Diego. This course will take you well clear of coastal dangers, traffic out of San Diego, and fishing boats operating inshore. Your navigation is more straightforward, and the skipper may sleep better at night. The inshore course may give you a light offshore breeze in the small hours, but more headaches. Northbound, plan to stay inshore, motoring N from Ensenada during the night hours, clearing Customs at San Diego in the morning, then making your way up the coast with as many stops as you wish. No safe anchorages or ports exist between Ensenada and San Diego on the mainland. It's best to count on a non-stop passage, however uncomfortable it may be. Unless you are lucky, it will be a windward trip, so plan accordingly. There have been occasional Ensenada races where the returning fleet has been able to run N in front of an aberrant SE wind, but they are rare as genuine Napoleon brandy (and have the same spiritual effect). Sometimes, the N-bound current will give you a mile or so if you stay inshore, too.

DANA POINT
(Chart 18746; *Chart Kit*, p.29; *ChartGuide*, pp.R1-2)

The coastline changes character S of Newport, as the rolling hills of the Irvine Ranch run down to the beach. Dana Point is conspicuous 12 miles S, beyond the sprawling buildings of Laguna Beach. The headland is the seaward end of a high ridge that ends in a brown sandstone cliff 220 feet high. San Juan Rock, a ten-foot high spur, lies 340 yards S of the cliff. Keep at least a mile offshore, and pass outside the red whistle buoy "2" (Fl. 2½ sec.).

Dana Point harbor was finally completed in 1976, and lies immediately SE of the cliff. The breakwater runs parallel to the shore and is easy to spot from seaward. Enter between the two breakwater heads, making sure you pass clear of the rock (7½ feet) and sewer outfall off the entrance, clearly marked on the chart. If you leave buoy "4" nearby to starboard entering, you will be clear of danger. Be careful, too, not to swing sharply around the end of the breakwater in case someone is coming the other way. Once inside, follow the bifurcating channel to either the E or W basin. The harbor office lies to port of the E basin entrance, and you should apply there for a slip (714) 496-2242, on Channel 16, then 12. There are two private marinas. A night approach is easy once you identify the light (Fl.G 5 sec) on the S breakwater, visible 12 miles away radiobeacon (... .... DP) is on 292 kHz. Dana Point is an excellent all-weather harbor, but exercise care entering during strong SE conditions.

Dana Point Harbor showing general layout of marina breakwaters.

Photo: AERIAL EYE INC., IRVINE, CALIFORNIA

DANA POINT TO OCEANSIDE
(Chart 18774; *Chart Kit,* p.31; *ChartGuide,* pp.R3-4)

S from Dana Point to San Mateo Point 6.5 miles away, the shoreline is still rugged and fairly high, with both the railroad tracks and the highway running close to shore. San Mateo Point is 60 feet high and lit (Fl. 5 sec. 15 miles), a fairly prominent landmark. But the most conspicuous signposts are the white domes of the San Onofre nuclear generating plant, 2½ miles S. The plant is brilliantly lit at night. Stay at least 1.5 miles offshore between Dana Point and Oceanside to stay clear of outlying dangers and kelp. The low-lying coastal plain between San Onofre and Oceanside is part of Camp Pendleton Marine Base. US 101 runs parallel with the beach. Keep outside the 10-fathom line on this 12 mile passage.

• **Oceanside harbor** lies just S of Santa Margarita River, which is crossed by conspicuous freeway and railroad trestles. An elevated water tank is situated 1.7 miles NE of the harbor. Approaching from N, you can steer for this structure until you locate the breakwaters. From S, identify the city pier. The harbor entrance is 1.2 miles NW and located just SW of a 17-story apartment complex painted white with a blue trim. Some considerate souls have even placed a sign saying OCEANSIDE on a hill behind the harbor.

The two breakwaters enclose the entrance, the E jetty bearing a light (Fl.R 5 sec) visible for 12 miles. Oceanside radiobeacon broadcasts on 323 kHz (--- .... OC). Two harbor basins are protected by the breakwaters: Camp Pendleton's Del Mar Basin and Oceanside harbor itself. A bifurcating dredged channel leads to the inner harbors; follow starboard fork to Oceanside harbor. Stay well clear of the rock groin on the port side of the entrance. Both ends are obstructed or shallow at low water. The other basin is government property. The harbor office lies by the turning basin. Transients should report there for slip assignments (714) 722-1418. All reasonable facilities.

Oceanside is reported to be difficult to approach at night. First-time visitors are advised to call the harbor office on Channel 16, then 12, for guidance.

OCEANSIDE TO MISSION BEACH
(Charts 18774, 65; *Chart Kit,* p.32-33; *ChartGuide,* pp.R6-T7)

I always find the next stretch of coast somewhat monotonous. From Oceanside you pass mile after mile of low tableland with steep and low, usually brownish cliffs that range between 60 and 130 feet high. The cliffs are dissected by numerous canyons that break the monotony of the bluffs. The railroad and US 101 run parallel to, and just inshore of, the beach. You can hear the traffic for miles to seaward on a still night.

The few landmarks on this long stretch of coast are:

• **Carlsbad,** 30 miles N of Point Loma: a conspicuous power plant stack with fixed and flashing red lights at night. A lighted bell buoy (Qk. Fl. W) and a complex of mooring buoys lie about a mile offshore. Your course should pass well offshore of this buoy.

• **Del Mar,** 18 miles N of Point Loma, a conspicuous smoke stack, also resort buildings.

• **A measured nautical mile** 13.5 miles N of Point Loma, marked by two pairs of steel towers.

• **Scripps Institution of Oceanography** lies 12 miles N of Point Loma. This famous institution is 5 miles S of where the coastal cliffs rise to about 300 feet and US 101 diverts inland. The Scripps buildings and its privately maintained pier are prominent from a considerable distance. A restricted area lies off the pier, and is clearly marked on the chart.

Point La Jolla is a ridge of Soledad mountain, a rounded, 822-foot high promontory that lies 9 miles N of Point Loma. It's easy to identify as it is the first high ground seen as you approach San Diego. The mountain has two TV towers on its summit. Buildings of La Jolla and Pacific Beach are prominent. When bound between Point La Jolla and Point Loma, keep at least 3 miles offshore to avoid extensive kelp beds that mask the rocky shoals inshore. A safe course along this 11-mile stretch takes you well outside the 10-fathom line.

MISSION BAY (Chart 18765; *Chart Kit,* p.33; *ChartGuide,* pp.T5-6)

Mission Bay entrance is 5.5 miles N of Point Loma and should be approached from well to seaward, even when coming from San Diego. From N, locate the US Navy Electronics Tower a mile NW of the entrance jetties (2 Qk. Fl. 7 miles). By this time you should see the 338-foot Sea World tower 1.8 miles E of the entrance. From S, the Ocean Beach fishing pier will be spotted 0.3 mile S of the entrance. Approach the jetties from seaward, and stay closer to the N jetty if any swell is running, as breaking can occur on the S side of the channel. Swells can break in 20 feet even in moderately rough weather.

Mission Bay is definitely NOT a harbor to enter during SE gales or heavy weather. Go to San Diego instead. At night, the N jetty is lit (Fl. 5 sec. 15 miles) and will be spotted first: the Fl.R 2½ sec. of the S. jetty is only visible 6 miles. Mission Bay radiobeacon operates on 317 kHz (-- -.-. MB).

The dredged entrance channel carries 14 to 19 feet and leads to Quivira and Mariners' Basins, on the E and W sides of the fairway. Several privately owned marinas in Mission Bay offer transient slips if available. Consult *Pacific Boating Almanac* or *ChartGuide for Southern California*. I have always had good luck at Mission Bay Marina (714) 225-9627.

If you want to explore the inner reaches of Mission Bay, do so from your dinghy. You can carry 6 feet and a 35-foot mast under the first fixed highway bridge as far as Dana Basin. Take *ChartGuide* with you. There is every facility for yachts in Mission Bay, but be warned that a surge can run into the harbor and the yacht basins in rough weather.

POINT LOMA AND SAN DIEGO
(Charts 18772-3; *Chart Kit,* p.34-37; *ChartGuide,* pp.T4, T7-10, U1-6)

The N approach to San Diego means closing with Point Loma. You should give a wide berth to the coast NW of the point, and approach at least 2 miles offshore to avoid kelp beds and New Hope Rock, 2¼ miles NW of the headland. George Davidson: "Vessels bound from the northwest make the ridge of Point Loma as a long, flat-topped island when about 25 miles distant." The lowlying ground behind the point will become apparent as you close San Diego. Point Loma is about 400 feet high, a rugged peninsula bare of trees but covered with sparse vegetation. US Pilot: "The tanks and buildings of a sewage treatment plant are conspicuous about 0.9 mile N of the point." The light is exhibited from a skeleton tower (Fl. 15 sec. 23 miles) and a radiobeacon (.-.. L) broadcasts on 302 kHz. The S approach will bring the lowlying coastline S of San Diego to starboard, and the higher ground of Point Loma between the Coronado Islands and the coast ahead. The highrise buildings of downtown San Diego are visible from a long distance to the S. A course towards the higher ground will enable you to identify the approach buoys from a comfortable dis-

Point Loma from S, with buoy no. 3.

Photo: JIM GRUENWALD

The coastline from Mission Bay to Point Loma, including San Diego harbor entrance.

Photo: AERIAL EYE INC., IRVINE, CALIFORNIA

tance. A night approach is made easy by the powerful lighthouse and well-lit entrance channel.

San Diego has been a favorite haven since Juan Rodrigues Cabrillo sailed into the entrance in 1542. The Presidio and Mission were founded as early as 1769. "Next to San Francisco, no harbor on the Pacific coast of the United States approximates in excellence to that of the bay of San Diego," wrote George Davidson in 1858. Early visitors to the bay, like Vancouver, anchored "in ten fathoms water, fine sandy bottom...The Presidio of San Diego bore N21E distant 3.5 miles, and the nearest shore north west, within a quarter of a mile of our anchorage." The entrance was first lit with a lighthouse on Point Loma on November 15, 1855, with a fixed white light of the "third order of Fresnel." Everything has become much more sophisticated since then.

Approaching Point Loma from N, give the headland a wide berth and aim to pass just outside the kelp, which can extend out as far as 2 miles. Whistle buoy "1" and bell buoy "3" mark the outer limits of the seaweed in normal conditions. Once past buoy "3," Ballast and Zuniga Points will open up, and buoys of the dredged entrance channel be identified. The limits of the dredged channel are marked by red and green flashing buoys (see Chart 18773). Arriving from S, you should head for Point Loma, then alter course for the entrance channel as the buoys come into sight and Zuniga Point is identified. Beware of becoming involved in kelp beds off Loma.

The entrance itself is straightforward. Tidal streams ranging between 0.5 to 3 knots set through the channel depending on the state of the tide. To time your entrance most effectively, make use of the Daily Current Predictions published annually in the *Pacific Boating Almanac*. Look out for a cross-current off Ballast Point that can deflect you into the channel. When S of Zuniga Point, you may experience a set towards the jetty on the ebb. Give yourself plenty of room. Keep a sharp watch for commercial shipping and warships in the dredged channel. They have right of way. Steep swells can form in the channel during SE gales.

In Davidson's day, the entrance was less developed. You entered watching the breakers on the shoals S of Zuniga Point. His sailing di-

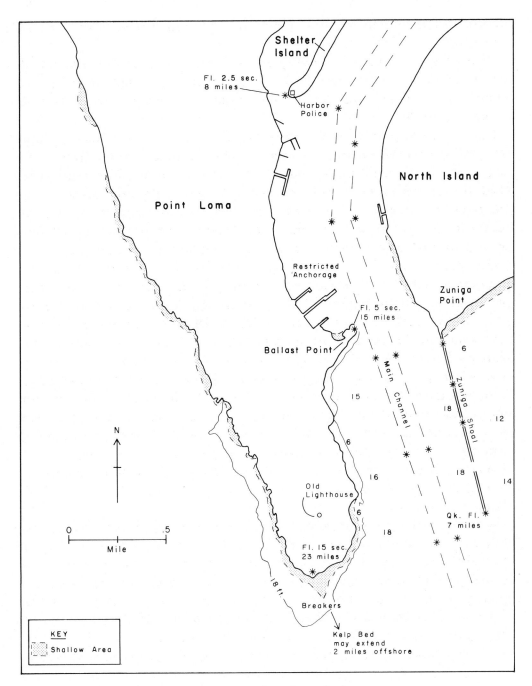

San Diego harbor channel plan.

rections for a summer transit cannot be bettered for a yacht drawing 6 feet:

"During the summer, keep as close to Point Loma as the draught of the vessel will permit, and lay on the wind up to Ballast Point, of which four fathoms can be carried within a ship's length, with ten fathoms in mid-channel."

There is a degaussing range near Point Ballast, so look out for ships engaged in demagnetizing operations. The entrance slowly trends to NE, with naval facilities to port and a measured mile to starboard. The entrance channel is well marked day and night and presents no problems for small craft. A night entrance is assisted by Point Ballast light (Fl. 5 sec. 15 miles) which should be kept on the port bow. Keep a sharp look out for the submerged old jetty to starboard.

The main yacht harbors and facilities lie opposite North Island and full details will be found in the *ChartGuide for Southern California*, pp. U1-4, and in the *Pacific Boating Almanac*. The harbor police office is at the W end of Shelter Island. Here that you can clear customs and obtain information about marina berths. Visitors' slips can be difficult to find in San Diego. Your best advice is to contact a private marina, or to make arrangement with one of the yacht clubs. You must, however, be a member of another club to qualify. For customs and immigration, call ahead to the harbor police on Channel 16, then 12, or telephone (714) 293-6356. Service: 0700 to 2000. Anchorage is permitted in San Diego harbor both in designated areas and elsewhere, but you should consult the harbor police first. Incidently, a light (Fl. 2½ sec.) marking the W end of Shelter Island is conspicuous (visible 8 miles).

San Diego harbor is enormous, and a fascinating place to explore both in your yacht and in dinghies. As with other large harbors, we recommend you carry *ChartGuide* and its large scale annotated plans aboard. All facilities for yacht maintenance and repair can be found.

You can enter and use San Diego harbor in almost any weather, which is a great convenience. Fog can hamper night and morning passage between September and April, causing sharply reduced visibility, especially in the entrance. Beware, too, of local wind variations that can cause drastic shifts within short distances. A final word of caution: San Diego is a commercial and Naval port. You must be prepared to give way to large ships and Naval craft operating in restricted waters.

SAN DIEGO TO ENSENADA
(Chart 18022; *Chart Kit*, pp.40-42; *ChartGuide*, pp.V1-10)

This is not a book about Mexican cruising, but many California yachts make an yearly pilgrimage to Ensenada as part of the annual Newport to Ensenada race each May, or make the harbor their port of entry for a longer cruise down Baja and into the Sea of Cortes.

The passage from San Diego to Ensenada is a pleasant downwind run that takes about 12 hours at 5 knots. Shape your course to pass inside the Coronados and follow the general trend of coast to SE. You will probably find yourself gybing several times, but are unlikely, under normal conditions, to experience a wind of more than 20 knots. Most yachts tend to hug the coast past Punta Salsipuedes, enjoying the rugged scenery that leads to Bahia Todos Santos and Ensenada. Make the southbound passage a day trip, planning to leave San Diego after an early breakfast. With normal winds, you will be enjoying margaritas at Hussongs that evening. The northbound passage is best executed during the calm night hours, under power. Stay at least 5 miles offshore and follow the coast, passing inside of the Coronados. If you leave after dinner, you should be in San Diego before the midday winds get up.

From the San Diego entrance, the coast forms a large, lowlying sandy bight as far as the border. The buildings of Imperial Beach are prominent, so is a fishing pier extending 1.5 miles from the city. If you follow the coast closely, keep outside the 10-fathom line as far S as Punta Salsipuedes. The US-Mexican border is marked by a white marble obelisk 4l feet above the water near a low bluff, 200 yards from the beach. The obelisk is 10 miles, 127 degrees M from Point Loma, and is aligned with a stone mound 1 mile E to form a useful line bearing. The circular, concrete bull ring just S of the border is also prominent. As a matter of interest, bull fights are held every Sunday from May to September.

THE CORONADO ISLANDS (ISLAS LOS CORONADOS)

These islands lie 15 miles S of Point Loma. They are 7 miles off the coast and are Mexican owned. These four islands make a fine landmark when approaching San Diego from the S. The celebrated British sailor Peter Pye was by here in the mid-1950s and described them as "round dry humps sticking steeply out of the water," an apt description. The Coronados are a favorite day excursion for San Diego yachts, and an underwater sports paradise. They extend NW for 4.5 miles and are surrounded by dense kelp beds. The cruising yacht is best advised to anchor at one of several fairly exposed anchorages:
• **Coronado del Norte**. A deep water island, but anchorage is possible off a lobster shack on NE shore. Be prepared to move out in a hurry if the wind gets up.
• **Puerto Cueva** on the E shore of Coronado del Sur, where there is 25 feet, sand, but considerable surge. The cove can be identified by the northern light (Gp. Fl 3 15 sec. 11 miles) on its S shore.
• **Old Hotel anchorage** on E shore of Coronado del Sur offers shelter from NW winds off an abandoned hotel/casino, a low, 2-story building at the water's edge. Anchor in 35 to 50 feet, rock and sand. Lay plenty of scope.
All Coronado anchorages are dangerous in Santa Ana conditions. You must have fishing permits or official papers to land in the Coronados. Another word of caution: avoid approaching the islands at night. The only lights (which can be unreliable) are on the southern island, the S tip being marked by Gp Fl. 2 sec. visible for 20 miles. A visit to these fascinating islands is best timed for quiet, NW weather in summer, when conditions are predictable. The seas can be quite rough off the Coronados in post frontal winds, especially around the southern light. Further information can be obtained from *Baja Cruising Notes*, published by Willamette Pacific, P.O. Box 6350, San Diego, CA 92106, or from the *Baja Sea Guide*, Sea Publications, Newport Beach, 1969.

The mainland coast between the border and Punta San Miguel at the entrance to Bahia Todos Santos consists of barren hills and bluffs, with cliffs as high as 80 feet. Behind are low foothills and dry mountains rising to over 3000 feet above sea level. This stretch of coast is becoming more developed. Here are some useful landmarks:

• **Table Mountain**, a conspicuous, flat-topped hill, 25 miles SE of Point Loma and 6 miles inland.

• **El Rosarito** is a small resort community some 12 miles S of the border. A refinery with 13 storage tanks and a power plant with 4 smoke stacks are prominent just N of the town. The Rosarito Beach Hotel is also conspicuous.

• **Punta Descanso** is the seaward end of a 392-foot high bluff, with an offlying 13-foot rock, Pilon de Azucar, 4 miles SE, sometimes referred to as Sugarloaf Rock. Although fishing boats anchor S of the rock in deep water, there is no reason to approach this stretch of coast closely.

• **Punta Salispuedes** is lower lying and is best identified by the large and well-lit mobile home park situated at the point. This is about the southern limit of coastal development.

Between this landmark and Punta San Miguel, the coast is barren and unlit, with higher rocky bluffs crowding on the shore. You can stay well inshore by day if you wish, and can anchor with some shelter from NW behind El Pescadero if waiting for calm winds when northbound. Punta San Miguel is bold and 150 feet high (Gp. Fl 2½ sec. 15 miles). The N shore of Bahia Todos Santos is backed by 50- to 100-foot cliffs and high hills. Keep at least 1.5 miles offshore between El Pescadero and Punta del Morro to clear kelp beds, breakers, and off-lying dangers. A course of 118 degrees M from a position that distance off El Pescadero will take you clear of dangers. Do not try to pass inshore of the kelp off Punta Morro. By this time you will see Ensenada harbor ahead. Punta Ensenada is 370 feet high, with a hexagonal house and mast on its slopes. The harbor breakwater extends SE from the point. A 150-foot chimney and a tank are conspicuous behind the town.

ENSENADA HARBOR
(Chart 21021, *Chart Kit* pp.40-42; *ChartGuide*, pp.V3-6)

The Port is easy to approach from NW, once you have identified the major landmarks. Steer for a point about a mile off the end of the breakwater (about 256 degrees M from a safe point off Punta Morro), then shape your course inside the harbor, keeping a close lookout for departing traffic, especially at night.

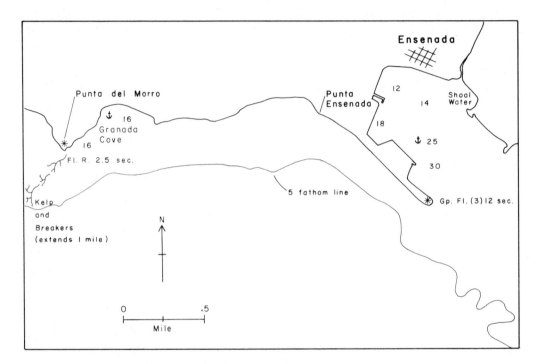

Ensenada harbor and approach.

The northbound yacht will approach from the vicinity of the Todos Santos islands, either passing outside San Miguel Shoal or S of this dangerous patch well clear of NW island. A short cut brings you between the Todos Santos Islands and the mainland, clear of off-lying dangers off Punta Banda, where strong N currents are reported. All these approaches should be taken with caution at night, as the lights are sometimes expunged. Todos Santos light (Fl. 12 sec. 22 miles) is reported unreliable. Its radiobeacon broadcasts on 292 kHz (_ ... TS). Punta Banda lighthouse is Gp Fl. WR (2) 8 miles. The SW shores of Bahia Todos Santos are steep and rugged, but the land S of Ensenada is low-lying and sandy. A number of excellent anchorages on the E shore of SE island, are well described in *ChartGuide*, pp. V7-8. Ensenada harbor lies 8.4 miles E of this island.

Ensenada is a commercial port, with no slips for deep water yachts. You must anchor off, in the shelter of the breakwater, in the area between the city waterfront and halfway to the breakwater. The holding is hard sand and mud, 15 to 30 feet. Some moorings can be rented. This berth can be crowded, especially at Ensenada Race time. Lay plenty of scope and buoy your anchor, and look out · for submerged objects.

If the harbor is too full, you can anchor in Granada Bay just E of Punta Morro in 15 to 18 feet, sand and kelp. Sound your way carefully into the cove, and expect some surge. This anchorage offers some shelter in prevailing conditions. Anchorage may be obtained on the S side of Bahia Todos Santos in SE weather, or in Bahia Papalote on the SW side of Punta Banda in NW winds.

Ensenada is a port of entry for Mexico. The Captain of the Port's office is on the NW side of the harbor, Immigration and Customs just N, in the town. Land your dinghy at the waterfront, tying it to one of the docks. Tip someone to watch it if possible, and avoid unlit areas at night. Facilities for yachts are somewhat limited. Fuel is obtained by jerry can from city gas stations, or by drum by prior arrangement. Details of facilities and services can be found in *ChartGuide* and the *Pacific Boating Almanac*, revised annually. *Punta Banda to Bahia San Quintin* (Charts 21021, 21003 or 4, 21041, 21061, *ChartGuide* pp. V9-W4), for those planning passage farther S, is covered in detail by *ChartGuide for Southern California.*

ENTERING MEXICO

Ensenada is the normal port of entry for Baja cruises. Before you leave the US, arrange for a customs agent to obtain consular clearance papers for you. These papers, fundamentally a crew list, have to be processed at a Mexican Consulate before you leave. The agents charge a fee, but it is well worth the expense. You can, of course, do the paperwork yourself, obtaining the forms at the consulate. Some chandleries carry supplies for the asking. The consulate certification fee is $8 for up to 9 people, $40 for over 9 (1980). Make sure you obtain the correct insurance coverage and fishing license.

Anyone visiting Mexico for more than 72 hours must complete a tourist card, obtainable on production of a passport or birth certificate from a consulate, or at Mexican immigration at Ensenada or the border. These are validated on entry.

Yachts on a Baja cruise must take these documents to the Captain of the Port, Immigration, and Customs at Ensenada between 0900 and 1400 weekdays. The customs will issue a temporary cruising permit and stamp tourist cards.

You must get the same papers stamped when you leave Ensenada, whether bound for a US port or to another Mexican harbor. The same procedure is repeated at all Mexican ports of call, during office hours.

Of course you should take your State Registration Certificate or Federal Documentation papers with you at all times, together with your insurance policy. Note that most Southern California yacht policies end at Ensenada or Punta Banda.

Here are some useful addresses for obtaining documents:

Customs Agents

We have heard good reports of Romero Yacht Service, 1600 W Coast Highway, Newport Beach, CA 92663 (714) 548-8931. Also of Howard Hartry, Custom House Broker, 301 West B Street, Wilmington, CA 90744 (213) 830-1010 and Raul Martinez, 12601 Venice Blvd., Los Angeles, CA 90066.

Mexican Consulates

San Francisco: 870 Market Street, San Francisco, CA 94104 (415) 392-5554.

Los Angeles: 125 E Sunset Blvd, Los Angeles, CA 90054 (213) 624-3261.

San Diego: Central Federal Bldg, Suite 225, 225 Broadway, San Diego, CA 92101 (714) 231-8414.

Ensenada gives you a tantalizing sample of the fascinating country that lies S of our familiar California waters. A beer at Hussongs, or a Mexican dinner and mariachi bands, are a delicious part of western cruising life, a life that can give you everything from ultra-modern yachting harbors to unspoiled anchorages that are unchanged since Richard Henry Dana's day. Fair winds, smooth seas and...enjoy...

INDEX OF ANCHORAGES AND HARBORS

This index lists all anchorages, and harbors mentioned in the book. It does not cover major landmarks or navigational beacons.

ABOUT THE AUTHOR

BRIAN FAGAN was born in England and has been cruising since he was eight. He is a Professor of Anthropology at the University of California and a well known teacher of archaeology. His books on the subject include several textbooks and the widely acclaimed *The Rape of the Nile* and *Return to Babylon*, histories of archaeological discovery in Egypt and Mesopotamia. He is co-author with Graham Pomeroy of the *Cruising Guide to the Channel Islands* (Capra Press and Western Marine, 1979) and has contributed to *Sail, Sea, Pacific Skipper,* and other marine publications. Fagan has sailed thousands of miles in Europe, between Finland and Greece, as well as in the Caribbean and California. He, his wife Judy, and daughter Lindsay, sail for several months each summer in their 40-foot cutter.

Brian and Judy are cat lovers and won the Cruising Association's Hanson Trophy in 1975, for a cruise from England to Finland and back.

The research for *California Coastal Passages* started in 1967 and has continued ever since. This has involved thousands of miles of passage-making under a wide variety of conditions, and long hours of studying old pilot books and archives.

NAUTI-NOTES